T0329172

Cambridge Elements

Elements in Environmental Humanities
edited by
Louise Westling
University of Oregon
Serenella Iovino
University of North Carolina at Chapel Hill
Timo Maran
University of Tartu

THE ANATOMY OF DEEP TIME

Rock Art and Landscape in the Altai Mountains of Mongolia

Esther Jacobson-Tepfer

University of Oregon

CAMBRIDGE
UNIVERSITY PRESS

CAMBRIDGE
UNIVERSITY PRESS

University Printing House, Cambridge CB2 8BS, United Kingdom

One Liberty Plaza, 20th Floor, New York, NY 10006, USA

477 Williamstown Road, Port Melbourne, VIC 3207, Australia

314–321, 3rd Floor, Plot 3, Splendor Forum, Jasola District Centre, New Delhi – 110025, India

79 Anson Road, #06–04/06, Singapore 079906

Cambridge University Press is part of the University of Cambridge.

It furthers the University's mission by disseminating knowledge in the pursuit of education, learning, and research at the highest international levels of excellence.

www.cambridge.org
Information on this title: www.cambridge.org/9781108790086
DOI: 10.1017/9781108855518

First published 2020

A catalogue record for this publication is available from the British Library.

ISBN 978-1-108-79008-6 Paperback
ISSN 2632-3125 (online)
ISSN 2632-3117 (print)

Cambridge University Press has no responsibility for the persistence or accuracy of URLs for external or third-party internet websites referred to in this publication and does not guarantee that any content on such websites is, or will remain, accurate or appropriate.

The Anatomy of Deep Time

Rock Art and Landscape in the Altai Mountains of Mongolia

Elements in Environmental Humanities

DOI: 10.1017/9781108855518
First published online: February 2020

Esther Jacobson-Tepfer
University of Oregon

Author for correspondence: Esther Jacobson-Tepfer, ejacobs@uoregon.edu

Abstract: Petroglyphic rock art in three valleys of Mongolia's Altai Mountains reveals the anatomy of deep time at the boundary between Central and North Asia. Inscribed over a period of twelve millennia, its subject matter, styles, and manner of execution reflect the constraints of changing geology, climate, and vegetation. These valleys were created and shaped by ancient glaciers. Analysis of their physical environment, projected from the deep past to the present, begins to explain the rhythm of cultural manifestations: where rock art appears, when it disappears, and why. The material and this remote arena offer an ideal laboratory to study the intersection of prehistoric culture and paleoenvironment.

Keywords: rock art, paleoenvironment, geology, Altai Mountains, Mongolia

ISBNs: 9781108790086 (PB), 9781108855518 (OC)
ISSNs: 2632-3125 (online), 2632-3117 (print)

Contents

1 Introduction

At the far western edge of Mongolia are three remote valleys. They will here be referred to by the name of the locale or the river for which they are known: the hill of Aral Tolgoi and the rivers Tsagaan Gol[1] and Baga Oigor Gol. These are also the names of the extraordinary rock art complexes within the valleys.[2] Individually and together the complexes reveal the cultural and environmental anatomy of deep time at the boundary between Central and North Asia[3] over a period of several thousand years.

At present and throughout most of the year, the valleys are essentially uninhabited, too cold and windblown to tempt humans to settle into the few protected niches alongside slopes and draws. A few exceptions occur. At the western end of the valley of Aral Tolgoi are crouched the wooden structures of Border Guard Station #1, Mongolia's version of a fortified border at the edge of China and Russia. In the long valley of Tsagaan Gol, the only residents in winter include a few Uriankhai and Kazakh herder families huddled into snug wooden huts at the base of the valley's unstable slopes. And in the broad valley of Baga Oigor, even some of the hardy residents who earlier maintained petrol supplies at the tiny settlement of Kök Erik descend to lower elevations to escape the cold blasts coming down from the high mountain ridge. Otherwise, a few wooden huts nestled into protective folds along the valley are the only indications of a human presence through the long, cold months.

Except for the wind, these valleys are silent. Even now, few figures are seen in the valleys: a rider, perhaps, or a herder driving his animals to higher pastures. An occasional car or truck may make its way along the miserable tracks that serve as roads. The dark bodies of yaks and horses may be spied on the upper slopes, slowly making their way to the ridges. Other than those signs of life, the land seems empty. That immense emptiness and the absence of any sound but the wind would suggest to many that this part of Mongolia has long been off any beaten track, too far from centers of civilization to attract attention. A closer look, however, challenges that assumption. Scattered through the valleys are

---

[1] Throughout the following pages, certain Mongolian terms will be used rather than their English translations. These include *gol* (river), *salaa* (branch, stream), *uul* (mountain), and *nuuru* (mountain ridge).
[2] These three complexes, or properties, together were entered into UNESCO World Heritage status in 2010 as Petroglyphic Complexes of the Mongolian Altai.
[3] Throughout this discussion, North Asia will refer to the Eurasian landmass north of the borders of agricultural China and bordered on the west by the Altai Mountains. In this region, rivers flow to the east or to the north. Central Asia refers to the landmass bordered by the Altai Mountains to the east, the Tibetan Plateau to the south, the Caspian Sea and Khirghiz Steppe to the west, and the Siberian taiga to the north. Within this region, rivers flow inland or, in the case of the Irtysh, to the north.

complexes of carefully arranged stones: stone mounds, sometimes highly elaborated, stone altars, standing stones, and stone images – all attesting to the creative presence of humans at some time in the deep past. Even more persuasive of this ancient layer of life are the dense concentrations of rock art covering the slopes along the valleys. This material, petroglyphic in character,[4] lies over the surfaces of bedrock and boulders like pictorial brocade, tracing out the lives of ancient hunters, foragers, and herders over a period of at least 12,000 years.

The physical environment of the three valleys in winter helps to explain their somewhat desolate aspect. The valley of Baga Oigor is broad and utterly treeless, defined in winter by its stony, dry steppe. That of the lower Tsagaan Gol is even more forbidding, although in the upper valley fragmentary larch stands can be found on north-facing slopes. The winter valley of Aral Tolgoi would seem to be the most propitious, since larch forests cover the mountain slopes dividing Mongolia from northwestern China. But, at this edge of Mongolia, the snow piles up and cold wind is funneled down from the narrow river valleys to the west, making winter habitation virtually untenable, except at the border guard station. In contrast to the other two valleys, here there is little winter pasture to sustain large animals such as horses and yaks.

In the short warmer months, between June and September, when snow and cold wind alternate with sun-filled days, the three valleys assume a different aspect. The steppe landscape of Baga Oigor and the upper Tsagaan Gol become covered with rough pasture extending up to rich grassland on the surrounding ridges. Good pasture appears in a few areas of the Aral Tolgoi valley but these are too limited and too close to forests and high ridges to support a significant animal economy. It is really the valleys of Baga Oigor and Tsagaan Gol that reveal the importance of mountain steppe in the emergence of a pastoral life at the heart of Asia. In late spring and early fall, these two valleys become the main routes for herders driving their flocks to high grassland and tundra.

A map of the region (Fig. 1) indicates that the three valleys exist within the same northwestern edge of Mongolia and at approximately the same latitude (49' 0' 0' N). They all offer direct routes up to the knot of glaciated mountains called Tavan Bogd – the Five Masters – marking the boundaries between Mongolia and Russia and Mongolia and China. In many ways they share a similar topography, one that is, for the most part, cold, arid, rocky, and mountainous. All were shaped by glaciers flowing down from the mountainous ridge on the west over thousands of years. Despite that common origin,

---

[4] Petroglyphs are images or signs that have been pecked or engraved in the rock surface. Pictographs are marks and images that have been painted. Because of the nature of the climate in this part of North Asia, there are no surviving pictographs in the open air.

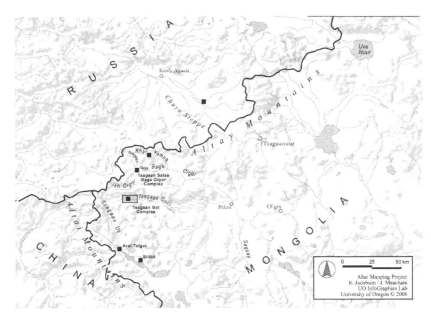

Figure 1 Map showing the location of the three complexes – Aral Tolgoi, Tsagaan Gol, and Baga Oigor – on the far western edge of Mongolia. (In this map, the Baga Oigor complex is referred to by its previously used name, Tsagaan Salaa–Baga Oigor).

Map: Altai Mapping Project.

however, and their geographical proximity, the valleys in question demonstrate that one geological rule does not apply to all: that the way in which ancient glaciers shaped one of the valleys was quite different from the others. As a result, the cultural legacy found in the three locations varied in ways that should inform our study of any open-air cultural traditions. In each valley the intertwining of human culture and environment has developed in different ways; and those differences over the millennia refer back to the complex and varied interconnections of geology, climate, and human culture.

Perhaps no single tradition more persuasively reflects the inextricable embrace of human culture by the paleoenvironment than the rock art in these valleys. It is not only that the pictorial subjects reflect layers in the evolution of human activities intersecting with changes in climate, vegetation, and animal life; no less vividly, each decorated panel reflects layers in geological time. Take, for example, a panel with the partial figure of an aurochs from Aral Tolgoi (Fig. 8). The animal was never completed: all we see are its powerful head and horn and its fore body, yet that summary image is enough to conjure up the live animal, its weight and power. The marks with which it was pecked recreate the deliberate gesture of the artist as he pounded the stone surface with direct blows. Deep and uneven, and originally white from the crushing of the stone, those pecked marks have returned to the coloration of the stone surface. This is a process of re-patination that requires thousands of years. The lichens beginning to fill the bull's contours also attest to a process that requires many years and the existence of climatic conditions that would encourage that growth.

The making of the aurochs' image is about process in time; but the most vivid sense of deep time is the stone surface itself. Its seemingly grooved character is an illusion: the stone is actually relatively flat. Those apparent contours are fossilized memories of a period when this material was part of a lake bed, washed and shaped into now frozen contours. Much later, perhaps millions of years later, and in the aftermath of enormous seismic changes, the lake bed was pushed up with the rest of Aral Tolgoi, ending at the very top of the hill. That was not the end of the geological process that underlies the aurochs' image. At some time in the late Pleistocene, glaciers came down from the high mountains to the west and covered the hill, polishing, grinding, and in some cases crushing its stone surfaces. This outcrop with the aurochs was never crushed but it was polished, scraped, and grooved. Thousands of years later, perhaps it was its unusual beauty that inspired some unknown hunter to begin his aurochs; but, however it came about, that creative process was aborted, and over the succeeding millennia the surface became covered with ground-hugging juniper totally hiding the aurochs until we found it in the course of our documentation of the hill.

The processes unveiled in an examination of the aurochs from Aral Tolgoi are not unique. They can be sought out with rock art in general and certainly with that of the Mongolian Altai. Their recognition challenges prevailing approaches to prehistoric rock art: the tendency to wrench imagery from the stone on which it is executed and from the climate and vegetation that shaped that ancient world. In considering the rock art of the Altai, it is essential to understand the rhythmic appearance of prehistoric imagery as a direct reflection of a fluid geology and climate; it is essential to return the rock art to its geological source – the stone itself and its ambient landscape.

In the following pages we will consider the coming of humans into each of the valleys with more specific detail. Here it suffices to indicate the general outline of that process as far as it is now understood. During the late Ice Age, hunters and foragers appear to have followed rivers and streams up into the high Altai from lower elevations, most certainly in search of large game and fish. Their numbers were certainly very few, but stone tool scatter and rock-pecked imagery indicate that they made temporary encampments along the largest river of this region, Khovd Gol. Following the traces they left in the form of worked stones and the images of large animals, we can imagine that they traveled upstream along the Khovd into the Oigor valley, possibly into the Tsagaan Gol valley, and certainly into the upper basin of the two lakes, Khoton and Khurgan Nuur. Scattered indicators of a human presence continued into what we call the Pleistocene–Holocene transition; that is the period between the end of the Ice Age and the beginning of our geological epoch (approximately 10,000–9,000 years ago). After that period, within the ensuing millennia of the middle Holocene (approximately 9,000–6,000 years ago), we lose sight of a human presence: not that people were not in that high region but that the signs of their presence have not been clearly identified.

That apparent absence changed, however, with the environmental transformations that began approximately 4,500 years ago, inaugurating our era, the late Holocene. The forests that had covered much of the mountainous region gradually disappeared, replaced by the expansion of mountain steppe vegetation into the highest valleys. With this transition, first hunters and then, slowly, herders reappeared in the valleys, seeking seasonal pasture and still abundant elk and ibex for game. By 4,000 years BP, these changes had catalyzed the gradual appearance of Bronze Age cultures in the high valleys. That process became fully manifested in the early second millennium BCE and lasted for more than 1,000 years into the early first millennium BCE. By that time – about 3,000 years BP – the physical environment of northwestern Bayan Ölgiy had settled into the dry, cold region with which we are familiar today and the Iron Age, characterized by a horse-dependent, nomadic pastoralism, had taken hold across the Altai and the Mongolian steppe.

In the present, the sheer emptiness of this world and its lack of any but a few minimal signs of human settlement do not alert the casual wayfarer to the ubiquitous indications of a rich cultural life in the distant past. Indeed, most modern travelers would not even notice these traces: they would move along the sides of the valleys heading (most likely) to the passes leading over the glaciered ridges of Tavan Bogd and into the high plateau and steppe beyond, their minds on anything but the darkened images that mark thousands of stone surfaces in these valleys. Were they to notice, they would surely be puzzled: where did these images come from, when were they pecked and engraved on the stones, what do they signify? And what was the significance of the elaborate stone altars, the rows of stone mounds, the great stele, and the occasional stone images of male warriors? In fact, this vast storehouse of imagery and surface monuments, this veritable art museum in the heart of Asia, reveals an anatomy of deep time, layers of human culture shaped by a radically changing environment over a period of more than 12,000 years. The physical environment of these valleys may be understood as the macrocosm of geological time, as process unfolding over millennia. The imagery pecked into the stone is a microcosm of change, the slow process of its creation and disintegration measuring the time of human generations. Between the two layers – that of the physical world and that of rock art – may be found intersecting patterns of location and elevation that reveal the rhythm and character of human habitation in the valleys.

The Study of North Asian Rock Art

Within scholarship on European prehistory, there is a well-developed consideration of the significance of location, view shed, and the human experience. A similar concern has characterized much of the modern study of the great rock art complexes of the Americas, Europe, Australia, and South Africa. Within Europe, much of that discussion relates to megalithic monuments but there are a few that consider rock art in terms of location, proximity, and patterns of human habitation.[5] By contrast, there are almost no studies of North Asian rock art that have considered view shed and elevation as legitimate aspects of the rock art's significance.[6] As a result, one confronts the paradox of a cultural expression embedded in landscape and part of the stone itself but divorced from any consideration of its encompassing, natural context.

In contrast to the state of theoretical scholarship focused on prehistoric rock art of Europe, that relating to North Asian rock art earlier than the Iron Age is rare. What does exist relates primarily to the earliest images within the basins of Siberian rivers such as the Yenisei, Angara, and Lena. This is at least partly the result of the very different character of archaeological remains in that cold and often desolate part of the world. The Neolithic as it existed in Europe did not occur in Asia north of present-day China: whether steppe or taiga or tundra, the land did not support agriculture except in very circumscribed regions, nor did it encourage the development of concentrated human settlements with all the social organization that implies. Within the mountain steppe regions of the Altai and Sayan ranges, the wind strips ephemeral materials and loose earth from the surface of the ground. This makes for a deflated cultural layer such that any cultural materials on the surface of the soil simply disappear or are displaced from their original strata. Perhaps the most significant impediment to the study of prehistory in North Asia is the fact that the only theoretical approaches were embedded in Soviet Marxist-Leninist constructions of the evolution of culture. One might say that the result was

---

[5] See, e.g., Jones et al. 2011, Helskog 2014.
[6] The most immediate exception may be found in Jacobson-Tepfer, Meacham, and Tepfer 2010.

a scientific tradition constrained by very narrow interests and approaches. On the other hand, now that the Soviet juggernaut has been released, the opportunity to explore the prehistory of North Asia is extraordinarily enticing.

In a somewhat similar manner, rock art within North Asia has been extensively studied but the vast majority of that material has been published in Russian or Mongolian and is thus difficult for Westerners to access. Much of that scholarly material, also, suffers from outdated approaches. The most extensive presentation of Altai rock art is associated with the Russian archaeologist, A. P. Okladnikov.[7] Recording thousands of panels and images along the rivers of North Asia, he and his colleagues established a tradition of reducing images to image types or typologies rendered in black and white silhouettes; alternatively he would reduce a panel, however complex, to black silhouettes on a plain white ground, thus effectively destroying the larger physical context. This method is somewhat parallel to the tradition seen in the study of southwest American rock art, where particular patterns in largely nonrepresentational materials are gathered into specific styles, for example, Carved Abstract Style or Palavayu Anthropomorphic Style, and presented removed from their immediate and larger contexts. In the case of the North Asian material, most typologies were simply generic (e.g., a single hunter) or they were never clearly associated with a style identifiable with more than the location of the site where the image was first identified. Thus, the "Angara" style of representation of moose and elk became rooted in the now destroyed imagery of that river, even though when analogous images appear elsewhere they might encompass very different stylistic characteristics.

Unfortunately, in the manner in which they cleaned and recorded rock art sites, Okladnikov and his colleagues essentially made further work on them very difficult. Furthermore, the approach Okladnikov established was wholly inadequate for anything but a study of typologies. Images were taken out of their compositional and physical contexts and rendered in black silhouettes that could theoretically be mixed and matched to establish typological data. As a result, for example, the magnificent rock art of the Yelangash River in the Russian Altai was reduced to page after page of black imagery without any pictorial context.[8] More troubling is the fact that in order to make an image more visually evident or even to make something out of what may have been very little, images were scraped clean of lichen, chalked or repainted, or otherwise

---

[7] For an extensive review of relevant materials published in Russian and Mongolian, see Jacobson 1993 and Jacobson-Tepfer 2015.

[8] Examples include all of Okladnikov's publications on rock art of the Yelangash Valley (1980, 1981, 1982) and his publication of the important petroglyphs of the Chuluut Gol in Mongolia (1981).

defaced.[9] Fortunately, in the last few decades, younger scholars have offered much more sensitive rock art studies, where the site is more carefully recorded and embedded in its natural environment. Nonetheless, many of the old methods of reproducing rock art imagery still pertain; and the general tendency to transform unique images and compositions into typologies is still dominant.

The problems inherent in such a typological approach can be quickly revealed. A large percentage of rock art imagery from the Baga Oigor and Tsagaan Gol complexes are embedded in compositions involving anywhere from 1 to 150 other images. While some of these panels may be simple conglomerations of images, most have what should be called a narrative significance: that is, the individual images are displayed across the rock surface and are postured so that they create a real sense of action and reaction or of change occurring in time, which is itself represented by the extension of space. A good example of how this works is offered by a hunting scene from Tsagaan Gol (Fig. 24), in which hunters on the right create a stampede of wild animals to the left across a space that we may imagine as a mountainous slope. A more complex narrative is found in another hunting scene, this from Baga Oigor (Fig. 44). In this composition, several hunters holding a variety of weapons encircle a bear; the posture of each hunter and the intrusion from the right and left of yet other running hunters conjure up the intensity of a scene from life. However, if these images were wrenched from their compositional contexts and reduced to image types, separately and together they would lose their narrative value. Similarly, if any of these images are presented as black and white drawings, they become divorced from critical signs of their geological context in space and time: the stone's texture and coloration become invisible, as do the scraped and abraded signs of a glacial past. In this situation, the rock art is removed from its given place; or perhaps it would be more correct to say that significant features of physical space and the indicators of a specific paleoenvironment are simply ignored.

Rock Art and Archaeology

Within the valleys that will be considered here, the cultural materials with the longest and deepest prehistory belong not to the great stone mounds and standing stones, but to the imagery pecked into the surfaces of boulders and bedrock. For better or worse, this material is often referred to as rock art, even

---

[9] These comments apply, in particular, to Okladnikov's recording of the great Lena River site of Shishkin (1959) and the cave of Khoit Tsenkir (1972). At many sites, e.g., Kalbak-Tash on the Chuya River in the Russian Altai, early researchers scrubbed lichen from the surfaces in order to trace the imagery. As a result, the stone surface was damaged and, of course, the lichen ultimately grew back.

Environmental Humanities   9

though many specialists refuse to consider it as having any discernible significance other than as a kind of pictorial commentary on the deep past. Since rock art in the Altai Mountains is either pecked or engraved into the surfaces of boulders and outcrops, it is petroglyphic in character. If there were ever pictographs (i.e., painted images) in the open air within this part of the world – and they may well have once existed – they have totally disappeared.[10]

Although rock art is usually included as a subfield within archaeology, its position there is not comfortable: unlike surface monuments and burials, petroglyphic rock art can be neither excavated nor directly dated.[11] Perhaps for that reason, or perhaps because most observers are not certain how to "read" the imagery, rock art rarely if ever enters into the investigations of archaeologists working in this area.[12] Even within scholarly studies of rock art itself, a critical consideration of dating is rarely engaged. As a result, the vast majority of studies of North Asian rock art have focused on imagery rendered as black and white drawings and in terms of typologies of subjects and styles. These are represented either as individual elements or within larger compositions; in either case, the imagery is divorced from the physical rock surfaces on which it is found and from the immediate spatial context of those surfaces. As a result, imagery becomes yet another archaeological data set, but one resistant to dating unless excavation archaeology reveals analogous realia. Images of wild fauna or domesticated animals can sometimes help to constrain dating, but, unless animal bones are preserved within burial sites or refuse pits, the imagery has no analogy within an archaeological context. Rock art of the Altai Mountains includes thousands of images of people wearing particular hats or clothing, but that material is ephemeral: one would rarely expect to find anything in burials or dwelling sites that might offer datable analogies. Within the Mongolian Altai, this silence is absolutely the rule with regard to sites or images earlier than the late Bronze Age (late second–early first millennia BCE). Exceptions to this cultural silence would be bronze or stone weapons or tools or even wooden weapons; but, while images of such objects do appear in Bronze Age rock art,

---

[10] The only surviving pictographs are found in caves; and, within the Mongolian Altai, the only major example of this cultural tradition is found in the cave of Khoit Tsenkir, in Khovd aimag (Okladnikov 1972).

[11] There have been a number of attempts to date petroglyphs scientifically, using a variety of techniques. None of them have thus far proved reliable. For one point of view, see Bednarik 2001; and see Roberts 2017 and Gibbon 2017.

[12] A recent study of several archaeological sites in northwestern China and western Mongolia includes one site with remarkable images of spirit figures. The archaeologists who investigated this site, however, ignored several critical questions that would bear on the dating and meaning of these images: whether there was an integral relationship between the excavated site and the covering stones with images; where those stones might have come from; and the possible relationship of these images to others found at distant sites. See Kovalev 2015.

actual examples in stone and metal are rarely found within a datable excavated context and examples of wooden weapons are nonexistent. This situation is fairly consistent across the Russian and Mongolian Altai and up into the Sayan Mountains in Khakassia.

The Petrology of Rock Art

Within the high Altai Mountains, cobbles, boulders, and bedrock will be either igneous or sedimentary in origin. In general, igneous granite appears in the form of freestanding stones ranging in size from boulders to gravel. Because this material emerged at the site of volcanic eruptions high in the mountains, one may refer to the large boulders as erratics (i.e., transported from their origin site, usually by glacial action). Granite is coarse grained, and in the Altai the coloration of the matrix is usually a mixture of gray, white, and black. Over the millennia, the weathered rind or skin of the boulder may frequently have acquired a dark brown coloration. When images are pecked into the granitic surface, they show up as white and stay that way for a very long period of time. Because of the damage to the outer layer of the stone, however, it is weakened and may subsequently peel or chip off, particularly as a result of freezing and thawing.[13]

Bedrock, by contrast, is primarily hard sandstone (greywacke), the result of ancient sedimentation in a watery environment followed by eons of compression and subsequent upthrust caused by seismic activity. Depending on the mineral content of the stone matrix, the surface coloration varies from dull brown to black, or from bluish green to a rosy-gold hue. Copper within the stone brings to the patina a bluish-green cast, black may indicate manganese, and red indicates a high ferrous content. Within the high valleys, which interest us here, that sandstone is frequently richly textured: with the scrape and gouging of ancient glacial action or with the suggestion of ripples created in the sedimentation of primordial sand. In certain areas, mudstone exposed for millennia acquires a satin-like coloration and texture. While in most cases it is probable that ancient rock artists pecked or engraved their images on any good stone at hand, careful consideration of the rock art in our three valleys indicates that in many instances, coloration and texturing may have persuaded an artist to use one particular surface rather than another. That is, the selection of surface may indicate something about individual discrimination in relationship to a larger physical context. Noting this is to become aware of a single person's taste cutting through the anonymity of deep time. At the same time, the rock itself reveals eons of a geological past.

The execution of petroglyphic rock art reflects an individual's intention and vision, that is, his particular stylistic understanding of the object or

---

[13] For an example of this process, see MAIC: PETR_00013_TG.

event he[14] wishes to represent and his muscular control of the process. The execution thus reveals manual gesture and the impact of an instrument on stone. In recognizing the process involved in making petroglyphic imagery, the observer returns vitality to otherwise inert marks and perceives the sign of a particular if anonymous person rather than that of a simple typology. In many cases, the pecked marks may not indicate any special artistry or accuracy; but, in other cases, the strength or clarity of the pecking and the refinement of the contouring edges convey a distinctive individuality (e.g., Fig. 43).

There are two ways of pecking out an image. In the direct method, the hammer stone is held by the artist and pecked directly onto the surface. Images executed in this manner are usually defined by rough and deep contour lines rather than silhouettes. In many cases, the resulting heavy pitting of the stone vividly conveys the impact of the hammer stone on the surface (e.g., Fig. 9). In the indirect method, the artist will hold the pecking instrument with one hand and hammer it with a heavy instrument held in the other. This second method offers much more control than the first; depending on the skill of the artist, it can result in pecked marks that are fine, shallow, and dense (e.g., Fig. 25). Within the Altai, images executed in the direct method may usually be assigned to a period earlier than the Bronze Age. Conversely, images that have been executed with dense, finely pecked marks and clean outlines were almost certainly carried out with indirect pecking using a metal tool or a very sharp and hard stone.[15] These should be dated within the Bronze Age or later.

It should be obvious that when rock art is presented in terms of black and white drawings, the very process of execution is lost; the character of the pecking – its force and precision – is fundamentally obscured. The same problem exists with regard to the character of the stone surface. Since the drawn image is removed from its stone setting, the coloration and texture, including the indications of glacial abrasion, are totally obliterated. And, if the artist of the image was attracted to one particular stone or another because of its texture or surface patina, those aspects of individual choice are lost. In thus reducing an image to a drawing in black and white, of course, its fundamental embeddedness in a physical, geological setting is lost.

---

[14] Throughout this discussion I will refer to the artist as "he," realizing at the same time that the individual could also have been a "she." On the other hand, given the fact that in all likelihood females were occupied with home-related activities (e.g., milking, food preparation, child-rearing), while males were involved with herding and hunting it is probable that most of the pecked images were made by boys or men.

[15] Of course, in all periods there were individuals whose pecked images were clumsy or inarticulate. For this reason, the simple identification of the means of execution does not assure dating. It does, however, constrain dating.

Consideration of a stone's surface coloration reasserts the interconnection of rock art and the natural world. Those varying tonalities are referred to as patina – the thin layer of coloration on the stone surface. In most cases the underlying sandstone is a dull brownish gray (e.g., Fig. 24), but the surface itself will vary in tone depending on a number of factors. These include the mineral composition of the stone, ambient dust, the proximity of the stone to vegetation, surface bacterial growth, and the slope and orientation of the stone surface.

When images are first pecked into stone, the resulting crushing of the rock crystals causes the images to come up white. That discoloration persists for centuries, even millennia, depending on a number of circumstances, all of which affect the speed with which the stone surface darkens or acquires its patina. One tends to assume that the older the rock art, the darker it will appear; and, although that is generally true, it is not a sure way to propose an approximate date. Generally speaking, the more vertical the surface on which the image has been pecked, the less the troughs and abrasions will retain moisture or dust; the more horizontal the surface, the more quickly the image will darken down. It has to be remembered, however, that when the images were pecked – and continuing for several centuries thereafter – they were far more visible in the landscape than they are now. In those areas where there is a singular density of petroglyphic activity from the Bronze Age – as is the case in the valleys of Tsagaan Gol and Baga Oigor Gol – the imagery could be said to have populated the slopes with people and animals. This condition is still highly visible in rock art from the Turkic Period (latter first millennium CE), particularly as it is clustered in parts of the Tsagaan Gol complex. That material, executed at least 1,300 years ago, is still white against its stone context: in one cliff area extending approximately 20 meters up the slope, the rock sections are covered with the whitish images of hunters and riders executed in the same period.[16] This section of the complex gives a vivid idea of what has been the appearance of many surfaces in the Bronze Age: dark stone covered with a great variety of animals and people, all white against their background. Now, however, those images have darkened and in many cases effectively disappeared. Only with careful looking and in a strong side light do they reappear.

Rock Art and the Natural Environment: Implications for Further Study

The basic identification of rock art sites and the systematic recording and publishing of those sites are the most fundamental approaches to an understanding of this

---

[16] Tsagaan Gol, section SK_H5; see *MAIC*: RA_PETR_TG_0625, RA_PETR_TG_0635, and RA_PETR_TG_0634.

material; they are the concerns that absolutely dominate studies of rock art in North Asia. If, however, one is truly to understand the material as a record of human culture, it should be studied within its own paleoenvironment: that is, within the interconnected geology, climate, and vegetation and faunal regimes characterizing that environment at the general time the rock art was executed. But those aspects of deep time were not stable: with every millennium they shifted, decentering the terms of human existence, forcing adaptations to new environmental worlds. Over the millennia, with the retreat of the Ice Age and the advent of a slightly warmer and moister environment, vegetation changed and radically so, thus bringing an end to certain animal species and favoring others. In the Altai, where the only economically viable activities had been hunting and foraging, with the spread of pasture land there gradually emerged opportunities for herding with all the social changes that that economy implies. Landscapes that had discouraged inhabitation became more inviting, at least at certain times of the year, and people began to come into the valleys first as individuals and families and then in groups. The physical world shifted and with it the way in which people experienced and represented their lives. Thus, the study of the human cultural layer should not be undertaken without a deep understanding of its physical context. Similarly, the imagery of rock art offers a window into the paleoenvironment, but one that is embedded in human perception.

The shifting past of the Altai valleys can be recovered by purely scientific means: the study of geology as it is revealed in stone and traced out in rivers, streams, and landforms, and the investigation of vegetation regimes locked in lake bed sediments. For the purposes of this study, one might think of the paleoenvironment as the macrocosm of time, the given stage on which social existence would have to be enacted; but it is the trace of that existence, and here most particularly the imagery humans left behind, that indicate human response and social change on the microcosmic level. Paleoenvironment and human culture are effectively two streams in the dialectic of deep time. In the case of the three valleys at the western edge of Mongolia, the consideration of both paleoenvironment and culture reveal an anatomy of humans responding to their physical world over millennia.

2 The Natural Context: Geology, the Paleoenvironment, Vegetation, and Fauna

The Altai Mountains extend from the Altai Republic (Russian Altai) in South Siberia down to the southeast, edging into northwestern Kazakhstan and northern China, and ending in Mongolia's Gobi Desert. The Altai are the highest mountains in Siberia: Belukha, within southwestern Russian Altai, rises to

4,506 m, while the Tavan Bogd knot of mountains at the boundary of Russian Altai and Mongolia rises to 4,356 m. Within the border region separating Mongolia and China and in the diagonal uplift separating Mongolia from China on the southwest are several major peaks over 3,300 m. Until the early twentieth century, many of these were still covered with significant glaciation, but that has changed radically over the last one hundred years.

The Altai uplift is one of several mountainous zones that arose as a result of the deformation of tectonic plates compressed between the Indian and Amurian plates beginning in the early Paleozoic (Shahgedanova et al. 2002, 314–326). The dynamic formation of the Altai accounts for the complexity and seismicity of its physical geography both within the Russian Altai and in the larger Mongolian extension. The northwestern region – northern Bayan Ölgiy, within which are found our three valleys – is high and characterized by a markedly disrupted mountainous zone. A satellite view indicates the Altai range trending from the northwest, in Russia's Altai Autonomous Region, to the southeast. Within Bayan Ölgiy, the physical geography has the aspect of knotted ropes studded with remnant lakes and threaded with small streams and rivers.

Elevations in the three valleys vary considerably, but all belong to the high mountain zone. Around Aral Tolgoi, the southernmost of our valleys, the elevation at the hill's base is approximately 2,103 m. while the hill itself rises only about 61 m above the valley floor. To the north and south, peaks measure over 2,443 m; just to the west, the mountains begin their rise to the elevation of Tavan Bogd. About 40 km north of Aral Tolgoi is the center of the upper Tsagaan Gol complex. The elevation of the valley floor there rises from approximately 2,300 m. to 2,560 m, while the elevation of the central, sacred mountain Shiveet Khairkhan is more than 3,200 m. About 30 km further to the north, the valley floor of Baga Oigor Gol is more gradual, rising from approximately 2,300 m to 2,400 m. To north and south, high ridges border the valley.

In the present, the weather in this part of Mongolia may best be described as continental, meaning that throughout most of the year it is relatively dry, cold, and windy. During the winter months, temperatures in the valleys under consideration can dip down to as low as -60' C. Spring months are windy and cold, while the short summer season lasts only two or, at best, three months. By August snow begins to fall intermittently in the high valleys. The mountainous ridge directly west of the valleys is the primary source of moisture in this part of Mongolia.[17] Within the huge, arid expanse of North, Central, and Middle Asia, and despite the radical retreat of glaciers due to climate change, mountain

---

[17] The Tavan Bogd ridge is also the primary source of the rivers and streams that flow down into northern China and beyond into Kazakhstan.

ranges such as the Altai still offer good grassland, high tundra, and some forest cover. Nonetheless, forest and good pasture continue to disappear with every year due to overgrazing and, most disturbingly, through the effects of global and regional climate change.

When this part of Mongolia was first explored and mapped by the Russian scientist V. V. Sapozhnikov (1861-1924), he paid particular attention to the glaciation on Tavan Bogd and bestowed Russian names on the largest glaciers; these names have persisted to this day (Sapozhnikov 1949).[18] Despite his pioneering work, however, within the study of North Asian physical geography and paleoclimate, the case of Mongolia has been relatively ignored. Most scientists examining these areas have been Russian; and with only a few marked exceptions, scientific studies have essentially ended at the border of Mongolia as if North Asia dropped off the map at that line.[19] Probably for geopolitical and economic reasons, scholarly attention has been devoted to the vast stretches of Siberia and to northern China and Tibet. With the important exception of the southern part of our region, centered on the lakes Khoton and Khurgan Nuur, there has been little interest in the remote northwestern corner of Mongolia. To a great extent, the geological prehistory of this region can only be inferred from the more certain outlines known for adjacent regions, i.e. northern China, Central Asia, and Siberia. This information, together with more specific information on the great lake basin (Khoton, Khurgan, and Dayan Nuur) and the northern Gobi, allows us to sketch out the character of Mongolia's northwest from the late Pleistocene down to the onset of the late Holocene and thence down to the present.

Glaciation and Impacts on the Human Presence

An understanding of the outlines of northwestern Mongolia's geological prehistory is essential if one is to understand the rock art of that region: its faunal subjects, its curious starts and stops over time, and the extent to which it reflects a deep glacial prehistory. In fact, the landscape of northwestern Mongolia everywhere bears the marks of extensive glacial action during the Late Pleistocene and down to the present.[20] In this part of Eurasia, Pleistocene glaciers took the form of high mountain icecaps with extensive advances

---

[18] The glaciers include the largest, the Potanin, named after the Russian botanist and explorer, G. N. Potanin (1835-1920).

[19] This is strikingly the case in the otherwise excellent publication edited by Maria Shahgedanova, *The Physical Geography of Northern Eurasia* (2002).

[20] There is still very little information on the glaciation of the Altai Mountains and Mongolia during the Late Pleistocene. For some relevant information, albeit regarding adjacent regions in Eurasia, see Velichko et al. 1980

down the intermontane valleys (Blomdin et al. 2014). As those glaciers retreated in the Pleistocene-Holocene transition, they left behind massive moraines and gravel-filled valley floors. The process by which these extensive moraines were built may have been complicated by a period of neoglaciation believed to have occurred during the middle Holocene (Herren et al. 2013). The resulting extensive glacial action over at least two periods of several thousand years is everywhere evident in the high valleys and on its stone: bedrock and boulders are marked by the scrape and gouging of ice rivers moving and shifting in several directions. It is also evident in the manner in which so much of the bedrock has been fractured into what are now collapsing cliffs.

The petrology of the high mountain region is dominated by finely grained sandstone formations, indicative of ancient sedimentary processes in the high valleys. At slightly lower elevations, the sedimentary stone takes the form of coarser-grained limestone. Scattered within this rocky landscape, sometimes in dense accumulations, are granitic boulders indicative of the most ancient igneous action in the mountain building process. Within the valleys that concern us, the dominant rock takes the form of either bedrock or massive boulders entrained by mountaintop glaciers and deposited high on the slopes or heeled into the glacial till of the valley floor. As a result of the rocky character of the landscape, rough vegetation in the valleys and along the slopes is thin and intermittent, while the high pastures are covered by tundra growth.

The last glacial maximum (LGM) for this part of Eurasia is usually dated between 26,000 and 19,000 years BP. That period saw the formation of steppe across Eurasia, characterized by extreme cold, drought, and in some places desertification. Across Siberia and regions of present-day Mongolia, alpine desert or steppe-tundra dominated, interrupted by small arboreal refugia. The region of northern China was characterized by extreme cold, grassland, and tundra, but without any glaciation (Goebel 1999).

Within Mongolia, the period referred to as post–LGM is dated between 19,000 and 14,400 years BP. At that time the climate slightly ameliorated, lake levels rose, glaciers receded, and steppe and forest steppe expanded. A following brief period, from 12,900 to 11,100 years ago, saw a return to very cold conditions accompanied by the re-advance of valley and mountain top glaciers. The onset of warmer and wetter conditions between 9,500 and 8,900 years BP marked the transition between the Pleistocene and the Holocene in northern Asia.[21] During the following millennia-long period, there was a significant increase in moisture: lake-levels rose again and forests expanded over mountain slopes. This period lasted until approximately 6,000 years ago

---

[21] Janz, Elston, Burr 2009; Barton, Brantingham, and Duxue 2007.

and the onset of the gradual drying trend that inaugurated the Late Holocene. By 3,000 years BP, the climate of northwestern Mongolia had reached its present-day character, which can be described as cold, dry, and dominated by steppe vegetation (Herzshuh 2005). These conditions reflect the fact that a broad region across Inner Mongolia, Xinjiang, and northern Mongolia is influenced predominantly by the trade winds known as Westerlies, in contrast to Yunnan and northern India, which are influenced primarily by the Indian monsoons. The extreme aridity in Mongolia and northern China resulted from the fact that mountain building in the Tibetan Plateau over the last 2.5 million years essentially blocked monsoonal moisture to the north and northeast (Guthrie 2001).

Vegetation Regimes

Khoton Nuur, the largest of three lakes lying in a trough paralleling the high mountain ridge bordering Mongolia and China, is a critical area in the reconstruction of northwestern Mongolia's paleoenvironment, particularly as it applies to the three valleys under consideration. A significant element in that reconstruction is played by palynology, the study of lake bed sediments containing many strata of pollens from regional vegetation. The study of such sediments at Khoton Nuur[22] can be triangulated with other studies in the region. These include analyses of lake bed sediment from the Ulagan Plateau of the Russian Altai (Blyakhachuk et al. 2004), from the Altai Mountains of Tuva (Blyakharchuk et al. 2007), from the Uvs Nuur Basin in Uvs aimag (Grunert, Lehmkuhl, and Walther 2000), and from Kazakhstan (Tarasov, Jolly, and Kaplan 1997). Taken together these studies confirm the outline of analyses of Khoton Nuur sediment.

Pollen concentrations from the Khoton Nuur sediment cores indicate that before 11,500 years ago, i.e. just previous to the Pleistocene-Holocene transition, vegetation around the lake was characterized by relatively treeless dry steppe with semi-desert vegetation such as *Artemisia, Chenopodiaceae,* and *Betula* (shrub birch). About 11,000 years ago there commenced a marked increase in *Picea* (spruce) and an increase of *Pinus sibirica* (Siberian and Sylvestris pine) (Rudaya et al. 2009). Between 10,000 and 8,000 years BP (i.e., the period including the transition into the early Holocene), the region became covered with boreal trees and open woodland, including shrub birches. Spruce-dominated forests slowly expanded to create a closed tree cover, and moisture-tolerant (mesic) vegetation gradually replaced xeric assemblages – those requiring a dry environment. This trend continued until approximately 5,000 years BP, by which time a decrease in moisture and lowered lake levels and temperatures resulted in the gradual replacement of spruce by larch (*Larix*) and pine (*Pinus sibirica*), the general retreat of

---

[22] Gunin et al. 1999, Tarasov et al. 2000, Rudaya et al. 2009.

forests, and the expansion of dry steppe. By 3,000 years BP, northwestern Mongolia had returned to a steppe environment in which the only extensive forests, limited to a narrow band along the Chinese border, are dominated by larch. Parallel to the early Holocene forestation and late Holocene deforestation visible across the region of the Russian and Mongolian Altai were patterns of forest expansion and then retreat south along the Altai ridge and down into the Gobi desert.[23] In that latter region, of course, the processes of desertification by the early first millennium BCE were far more pronounced.

In the present, the forests that once must have covered the slopes over Baga Oigor Gol have totally disappeared. In the valleys of Sogoogiin and Sagsay Gol[24], some remnant groves cling to high draws on north-facing slopes, while along the upper Khovd survive a few more extensive forested areas. The lower Tsagaan Gol valley is treeless, but in the upper valley scattered larch groves persist where animals cannot pass: on the unstable slopes on the north face of Shiveet Khairkhan and in small, high draws on north-facing slopes over Khar Salaa. The heaviest remnant forests are found on north-facing slopes bordering Khara Salagiin Gol, a tributary to Khoton Nuur; on the north facing slopes over Khoton and Khurgan Nuur; and, further to the southeast, in the valleys of Songinyn and Elt Gol. All of the now surviving forest cover is dominated by larch, though pine and willow can still be found in a few pockets.

Faunal Regimes

The vegetation and climate history of northwestern Mongolia can be directly correlated with specific animal species. The representation of those species, in turn, refers back to a necessary vegetation regime – the environment without which the species would not survive in the area. In speaking of both vegetation and faunal regimes and of the implicated chronology of climate and geology, it is essential to keep in mind that there were no sharp breaks in epochs, no clear line where, for example, late Pleistocene gave way to early Holocene. That necessarily gradual change in the paleoenvironment means, of course, that faunal species did not suddenly appear or disappear. Those transformations were certainly as gradual as we have been able to observe in our own environment, wherein a species – for example, polar bears – will slowly disappear from their previous habitat.[25] By extension, this model of paleoenvironmental change

---

[23] Miehe et al, 2007; Janz, Odsuren, and Bukhchuluun 2017, pp. 25-26.

[24] Oigor Gol flows into the Sogoogiin Gol, and thence into the Khovd. Sagsay Gol flows north from the Chinese border to enter the Khovd just before the main center in that region, the town of Ölgiy.

[25] Actually, given contemporary climate change, it is likely that changes in the Pleistocene–Holocene transition were much more gradual than what we see today.

can also be correlated with human habitation and social economy beginning in the late Pleistocene.

The model of environmental change I propose here allows us to propose a chronology of rock art in the valleys. We can divide the faunal species into three general groups: those that must be associated with the late Pleistocene and Pleistocene-Holocene transition; those that seem to have made their entrance in the early Holocene and persisted thereafter; and those we have to associate with the Bronze Age and later. While we speak here of faunal species, in most cases we have to depend on the rock art record in order to interpolate what is absent from the archaeological record.

A. Fauna of the late Pleistocene and Pleistocene-Holocene transition in north-west Mongolia that disappeared by the onset of the Holocene:

- In this group, we have to reconstruct the faunal regime through rock art records; in this process, however, we can find extensive material support in the archaeological excavations of caves in the Russian Altai.[26]

- Mammoth (*Mammuthus primigenius*). The most familiar of the megafauna inhabiting the cold Eurasian steppe during the late Ice Age. Their survival depended on hard ground and harsh, xeric steppe vegetation. Within the temperate belt of Siberia, late mammoth finds date to between 11,980–10,210 years BP, but across northern Eurasia extinction dates vary considerably.[27] Several images of mammoths have been identified in the Baga Oigor valley.

- Woolly Rhinoceros (*Coelodonta antiquitatis*). Within northern Eurasia, the woolly rhinoceros is believed to have occupied open, cold steppe during the Ice Age; but it was also dependent on browse such as willows and alders in shrubby thickets along waterways and sloughs. In northern Eurasia, the extinction of the woolly rhinoceros is believed to have occurred before the Pleistocene-Holocene transition: the most recent C14 date associated with rhinos is 10,700 years BP, from a site in West Siberia (Orlova et al. 2004, Kuzmin 2010). There is one image of a rhinoceros at Aral Tolgoi.[28]

---

[26] The caves in question include Strashnaya and Kara-Bom, *inter alia*. See Derevianko, ed. 1998, pp. 84–106.

[27] Mammoth ecology and survival in North Asia are complex, with indications that in some isolated areas examples of the species lasted until much later. The causes for the disappearance of mammoths from North Asia have been extensively debated, with some scholars insisting on the changes in habitat (climate, permafrost solidity, vegetation) attendant on the Late Pleistocene-Holocene transition; others argue that the final collapse of that species had as much to do with human predation as with long-term changes in climate and vegetation. See Vershchagin and Baryshnikov 1982; Vartanyan, Garutt, and Sher 1993; Martin 1982; Orlova, Kuzmin, and Dementiev 2004; Velichko and Zelikson 2005; Kuzmin 2010.

[28] *MAIC*: RA_PETR_AT_0055. There is a much later image in the Khöltsöötiin Gol complex, but it is impossible to correlate that image with the information on woolly rhinoceros extinction in northern Eurasia. See Kuzmin 2010.

- Aurochs (wild cattle, *Bos primigenius*). Wild ancestor of domesticated cattle. Considered to be among the Pleistocene megafauna, which either disappeared or evolved in the Holocene. Aurochs appear to have died out in North Asia long before disappearing from Europe. Rock art imagery from Mongolia indicates that aurochs ranged across dry steppe and in the steppe-forest interface through the Bronze Age. The aurochs was a grazer like its domesticated later form. Images of aurochs appear at all three complexes under consideration, but they seem to disappear before the late Bronze Age.
- Wild horses (*Equus caballus*; descendant forms = Przewalski's horse, *Equus ferus przewalskii* [Mongolian: *takhi*]). As grazers, wild horses were acclimated to a steppe environment and did not inhabit forestland. Orlova et al. (2004) state that within Siberia, *Equus caballus* seems to have disappeared between 11,700–9,000 years BP but reappeared about 4,600 BP, disappearing again in the northern part of its range by 2,200 BP. The trajectory of the wild horse in northwestern Mongolia, as documented in rock art, suggests a very similar prehistory: its disappearance in the early Holocene correlating with the expansion of forests and its reappearance correlating with the onset of the late Holocene, the retreat of forests, and the expansion of dry steppe. The Mongolian *takhi*, or Przewalski's horse, is now believed to be a direct descendant of the early domesticated horses associated with the Eneolithic Botai culture (Gaunitz et al. 2018). The takhi inhabited a wide region, from Central Asian steppe across the steppes and forest steppes of the Mongolian Altai into southern Siberia (Foronova 2006).
- Ostrich (*Struthio anderssoni*). Ostrich eggshell finds in southern Mongolia and northern China indicate that *Struthio* was native to the arid steppe and deserts of those areas (Janz et al. 2009). They co-occurred with mammoths, woolly rhinoceros, and horses, as well as with species that survived into a later period (e.g., aurochs, argali) (Deng 2006). The amelioration of climate in the early Holocene, with expanding forest, forest–steppe, and more humid steppe environments, would have gradually confined ostriches to more arid zones (Zhao et al. 2007; An et al. 2008). The only certain rock art images of *Struthio* in the open air are found at Aral Tolgoi.

B. Fauna that appear in rock art by the early Holocene and persisted through the Holocene and into historical times:
- Argali (*Ovis ammon*). The largest of all wild sheep, argali prefer gently sloping pastures at high elevations, but also inhabit high, rocky ridges. They avoid areas of deep snow, or graze in areas where winds blow snow

cover off the surface. Argali graze on grasses, sedges, and forbs, but will browse on low brush. Images of these animals are found at Aral Tolgoi, Tsagaan Gol, and Baga Oigor.

- Ibex (Siberian ibex, *Capra sibirica*). Grazers and browsers, ibex feed on grasses and sedges, spruces and willows. They prefer high open slopes and rocky ridges above the tree line, not forests; and they avoid heavy snow. Images of these animals are found at Aral Tolgoi, Tsagaan Gol, and Baga Oigor.
- Elk (Altai Wapiti, *Cervus elaphus sibiricus*). Elk inhabit forest and forest-grassland interface, but will venture out into open grassland for temporary feeding. Elk are grazers and browsers and, in many regions, migratory animals shifting between winter and summer feeding grounds. Many images of these animals are found at Aral Tolgoi, Tsagaan Gol, and Baga Oigor.
- Bear (Siberian brown bear, *Ursus arctos collaris*). Bear inhabit boreal forests and adjoining valleys with riparian zones. They are omnivorous, eating small mammals, fish, seeds, nuts, berries, and roots. Pre-modern images of these animals are found at Aral Tolgoi, Tsagaan Gol, and Baga Oigor.

C. Fauna that emerged only in the mid-Holocene:

- Moose (European elk, *Alces alces*). Moose are the largest of all cervids; they are browsers and dependent for forage on forests and riparian zones. Moose are more capable of handling heavy snow than are elk, but they are less tolerant of heat. In contrast to elk, moose are solitary animals. Images of moose appear in the Tsagaan Gol and Baga Oigor complexes.
- Wild yak (*Bos mutus*). Yaks are believed to be native to Tibet, from where they spread to neighboring high elevation regions also characterized by harsh vegetation, extreme cold, and snow (Rhode et al. 2007). The process of their domestication by nomadic pastoralists is unclear, but from *Bos mutus* evolved the domesticated yak (*Bos grunniens*) (Leslie and Schaller 2009). The date and circumstances relating to the existence of wild yaks in the Altai are also uncertain, but their presence in the mid-Bronze Age is attested by a few rock art panels from Tsagaan Gol and Baga Oigor. Images of domesticated yaks appeared only in the mid-Bronze Age.

D. Fauna that were represented in the late Holocene (late Bronze Age):

- Boar (*Sus scrofa*). Boars are omnivorous and depend on a variety of animals and insects as well as on the nuts, berries, and bulbs of forested areas. They are not adapted to snow. When they appeared in western

Mongolia is not certain, but with only one or two exceptions[29] they are represented only in the late Bronze Age and later.

- Domesticated yak (*Bos grunniens*). Not represented until the Bronze Age.
- Wolves (Eurasian gray wolf, *Canis lupus lupus*). Not represented until the Bronze Age.
- Dogs. Not represented until the Bronze Age.
- Snow leopards (*Panthera uncia*). Not represented before the late Bronze Age.
- Bactrian camels (*Camelus bactrianus)*. To judge from rock art representations, Bactrian camels were introduced into the Altai Mountains as pack animals only late in the Bronze Age. They are adapted to high, cold, and dry regions, but their migratory routes are determined by the presence of water. Poorly preserved paintings in the cave of Khoit Tsenkir, in Khovd aimag, indicate the presence of the wild species (*Camelus ferus*) in the late Pleistocene (Okladnikov 1972); these animals are now confined to a region in the Mongolian Gobi desert. On the other hand, the use of the domesticated Bactrian is ubiquitous in the Altai region.

E. Other fauna attested in rock art of the Bronze Age and later:
- Rabbits or hares
- Birds (including cranes, ducks and other water birds, a variety of raptors, and ptarmigan)
- Fish
- Snakes

The association between faunal species and environment in northern Eurasia, here including our mountainous region in Bayan Ölgiy, was analogous to faunal distributions within the Mongolian Gobi and northern China dry steppe regions (Janz, Odsuren, and Bukhchuluun 2017). Within the northern Altai and regions further to the north, faunal species were more characteristic of an at least partially forested landscape. The conditions within the northwest mountainous region may be summarized as follows. The cold steppe environment of the Pleistocene was characterized by extensive permafrost, aridity, and xeric vegetation interspersed with low shrubs and deciduous trees. Within that steppe environment, aridity and wind probably prevented heavy snow accumulations. Until the late Pleistocene, this environment supported mammoths, animals dependent on the harsh vegetation of the cold steppe and on extensive frozen ground (Velichko and Zelikson 2005). Similarly, woolly rhinoceros occupied

---

[29] One of the oldest and finest images of boars I have found in the Mongolian Altai is on a damaged surface in the locale of Khara Zharyg above Tsagaan Asgat Gol. See *MAIC*: PETR_00001_KV.

open, cold steppe, but were also dependent on the browse of wetter areas – browse such as willows and alders in shrubby thickets. Aurochs and horses were able to move between open steppe and open woodlands (Müller-Beck 1982); thus they could survive extreme cold and relatively dry environments. Like the larger animals, they would avoid heavy snow. Elk are grazers and browsers, best served in an environment where they can migrate out of snowy areas and forage between open grassland and protective forest zones. This means that the cold, frozen steppe that supported mammoths and rhinoceros would not have been propitious for elk. Similarly, although bears can forage in open grassland, they require forest for nuts, berries, shoots, and leaves, and streams for fish. Argali and ibex inhabit ridges, mountaintops, and high grassy slopes, and avoid heavy snow and forests. While East Asian ostriches are thought to have become extinct in the late Pleistocene, there is good evidence that they survived in Mongolia and northern China until well into the Pleistocene-Holocene transition (Janz, Elston, and Burr 2009). Ostriches inhabited dry, open steppe or semi-desert. Thus the environment that would have supported such animals as elk or bear would not offer habitat for ostriches. When we consider the interwoven aspects of climate, vegetation, and fauna, it becomes apparent that the study of rock art and its subject matter must be calibrated with the prehistory of vegetation and faunal regimes, set within the context of a changing paleoenvironment. In the study of rock art, faunal types in conjunction with the means and style of execution will often indicate a very particular paleoenvironmental niche. For this reason, it is not sufficient to simply identify an image – for example, argali, elk, aurochs – without also noting the manner in which it was executed, the larger compositional context (if any), and the specific means of its execution.[30]

3 The Complex of Aral Tolgoi

Although there has been extensive investigation of early human presence in northern and southern Mongolia, there is very little evidence for human habitation of the high Altai in the late Pleistocene.[31] It is probable that environmental conditions at that time and at that elevation discouraged an even seasonal hunter-forager presence except along the shores of certain rivers. Some perspective on this problem is offered by the greater understanding of the same period in adjoining regions. During the Late Pleistocene, within the upper Yenisei and upper Angara just north of present day Mongolia, glaciers were

---

[30] Approaches to the dating of rock art in the Mongolian Altai are elaborated in two previous publications: Jacobson-Tepfer 2015, 371–384; and Jacobson-Tepfer 2019, 99–116.

[31] For references to studies on Pleistocene sites in Mongolia, see Janz, Odsuren, and Bukhchuluun, 2017. Exceptions to the statement regarding the high Altai are finds from caves in the Russian Altai. See Derevianko, Powers, and Shimkin, 1998.

Figure 2 The hill of Aral Tolgoi, seen from the east, beyond Border Guard Station #1. Beyond Aral Tolgoi rises Ulaan Uul.

Photo: Gary Tepfer.

limited to alpine regions. The climate was extremely cold, dry, and windy. Vegetation took the form of pine forest steppe on lower mountainous elevations and treeless *Artemisia* steppes in the valleys.[32] All indications are that a similar environment awaited the hunters and foragers who ventured into the high valleys of the Mongolian Altai at the end of the Ice Age. The rock art in those valleys indicates, however, that the long-term fates of a human presence were different from valley to valley. The imagery recorded there serves as a primary document for investigating the intertwining of human experience and the paleoenvironment. An examination of this proposition can begin with the southernmost of our three complexes – Aral Tolgoi.

Aral Tolgoi is the name of a hill located at the far western end of Khoton Nuur. From the east the hill has the aspect of a long whale rising from a broad plain (Fig. 2). Beyond Aral Tolgoi to the west, the river valleys narrow and the mountains pile up to the boundary with northern China (Fig. 3). From the ridge of the hill looking east are visible the surrounding alluvial plain bisected by rivers to north and south and Khoton Nuur, into which they rivers flow (Fig. 5).

Originally Khoton Nuur and its neighbor to the east, Khurgan Nuur, were part of one giant lake occupying a great glacial basin at the western edge of Bayan Ölgiy. The geography of this basin reflects a process in deep time, when glaciers advanced from the higher valleys of Khara Salagiin Gol, Postigiin Gol, and the long valley of Rashaan Gol – the three rivers that flow into Khoton Nuur from

---

[32] Goebel 1999. The focus of Goebel's attention is Siberia proper, down to the border of Mongolia and Kazakhstan, but including the Sayan and Altai mountains within that region.

Figure 3 View west up the Khara Salaagin Gol to the border of Mongolia and China.

Photo: Gary Tepfer.

the west. Early glacial advances must be responsible for the huge moraines on the north side of Khoton and Khurgan Nuur as well as for the great terminal moraine at the southeast end of Khurgan Nuur. These are quite visible in a satellite image of the lake basin (Fig. 4); visible, also, are the banded slopes of the lateral moraines along Khoton Nuur. This and Khurgan Nuur are in effect remnant lakes. The visible strata of the north shore of Khoton Nuur indicate successive shorelines when the single lake that had filled the basin well above its present level began to recede. On the south side of Khoton Nuur, forested slopes rise steeply from the present day shoreline. The south shore of Khurgan Nuur is a crazy-quilt of eroded moraines leading into the huge curved shore of the terminal moraine.[33]

The glacial advance and retreat reflected in the larger physiography of the basin also impacted the hill of Aral Tolgoi, as if it were a microcosm of the larger lake region. Given the topography of this end of the basin, each successive glacial advance is certain to have covered Aral Tolgoi, gradually wearing its stone outcrops down to the surface of the hill and leaving the stone cracked and crushed (Fig. 5).

At the time of the last such advance, massive granitic boulders were entrained and deposed along the ridge or on the more moderately sloping west side. In the

---

[33] A third lake, Dayan Nuur, lies southeast of Khurgan Nuur, within a different drainage. However, it together with Khoton and Khurgan comprise the Great Lakes in this far edge of Mongolia.

Figure 4 Satellite view of the Khoton and Khurgan Nuur basin. Khoton Nuur is on the left, Khurgan Nuur is on the right. The whitened slopes on the north and east of the lakes indicate the height of the combined lake in the early-middle Holocene. Khovd Gol exits Khurgan Nuur on the far right, and Aral Tolgoi lies at the far western end of Khoton Nuur. Google Earth.

Figure 5 View from the top of Aral Tolgoi east to Khoton Nuur.
Photo: Gary Tepfer.

present, larch forest covers the north slope of Aral Tolgoi, obscuring any rock surfaces that may have once been visible. The south slope and the ridge of the

Figure 6 View east over Aral Tolgoi in the middle distance before Khoton Nuur. On the right are the forested slopes south of Khara Salagiin Gol and Khoton Nuur.

Photo: Gary Tepfer.

hill are now bare of vegetation. This pattern – forest persisting on north-facing slopes but absent on south-facing slopes – holds true of many parts of this larger region at the western edge of Bayan Ölgiy. It reflects the effects of harsh sun on the south sides and greater moisture and cold on the north sides.

The only known rock art in the upper valley of Aral Tolgoi and around the southern boundary mountains is limited to what appears on Aral Tolgoi itself. Of course, it is entirely possible that more images could be found on bedrock presently covered by surrounding forests; but if that were the case they would by now have been totally obscured or even destroyed by vegetation.[34] In the valleys further to the west and northwest of Aral Tolgoi, the forests have significantly retreated on all but the north-facing slopes, and occasionally there is considerable exposed bedrock (Fig. 6). However, a careful examination of many of these outcrops indicates that there are no images now and probably never were. On the other hand, across the valley floor, on the south side of Aral Tolgoi and within the narrow valleys of Khara Salagiin Gol and Postigiin Gol are many ritual and memorial monuments from the early Iron Age and the Turkic Period. Similarly, east of Aral Tolgoi, on three hills bordering the north

---

[34] We located one of the finest images at Aral Tolgoi (Fig. 8) on bedrock that had been covered by ground-creeping juniper.

shore of Khoton Nuur, is a large concentration of surface monuments and petroglyphs.[35] These seem to date to the late Bronze and early Iron ages and to the Turkic Period. In other words, cultural remains throughout the basin leading west to Aral Tolgoi and around that hill itself would indicate that after the early Holocene few hunters or foragers ever penetrated to the far end of the basin until the late Bronze or early Iron Age. This hypothesis is supported by surface monuments and by the rock art itself.

The Rock Art of Aral Tolgoi

The bedrock of Aral Tolgoi is a form of hardened sandstone, but its appearance and texture vary across the hill. This variation certainly reflects the specific mineralization of the local stone, but it also seems to depend upon location and the effects of differing pressure from glacial action and exposure to millennia of weather. The outcrops at the eastern base of the hill are deeply abraded and covered by layers of lichens. Along the ridge of the hill and on the south side of the hill as it slopes down to the level of the surrounding plain, some surfaces are remarkably smooth and polished while clearly bearing the traces of glacial scrape. In these instances images tend to be best seen in flair. At the top of the ridge, much of the bedrock is broken into multiple, crumbling sections (Fig. 5). In other cases the bedrock is grooved as if it were a molten stream. These sections may reflect what had once been lake bed sediment washed and molded by swift water and then, much later, uplifted in seismic activity and ultimately scraped by glacial action.

There are approximately thirty significant outcrops on Aral Tolgoi; most of these are relatively flat or close to the earthen surface. There are, also, a few outcrops of a more prominent nature particularly on the eastern end of the hill and in the case of the outcrop known as AT 13.[36] On twenty-seven of the outcrops can still be discerned partial or whole images. Across the identified, decorated outcrops there are approximately 170 images or groups of images; but this kind of a count is not very meaningful when one realizes that in many places the old images are simply illegible, lost in the crumbling of the surface and in the scrabble of lichen (Fig. 7).[37] While one might hope to discover more

---

[35] This is the site known as Bilüüt. To date, the primary publication of the petroglyphs of this complex is that by Richard D. Kortum (2018). While some of the images published in this book may be early Holocene, the quality of the reproductions makes that proposed dating uncertain. We have documented scattered petroglyphs in some of the high valleys south of Khurgan Nuur. On the basis of subject and style, these may be dated to the Bronze and early Iron Ages.

[36] The letters AT plus a number indicate the particular section on the hill as we mapped it.

[37] The image count offered here is derived from the drawings included in the only full publication to date of Aral Tolgoi (Tseveendorj, Kubarev, Yakobson 2005). I would urge caution, however, in using that as a reliable number, not only because so many images are essentially lost but also because whole compositions, sometimes with multiple images, are included as one drawing. In other cases, also, specific panels have been only partially recorded.

Figure 7 Ibex and two frontal stick figures. Pleistocene–Holocene Transition. Aral Tolgoi.

Photo: Gary Tepfer.

decorated outcrops on the north side of the hill, that is unlikely. Not only is that slope covered by thick forest, it is also true that in this part of the Altai, north-facing slopes are rarely decorated. By contrast to the bedrock, none of the granitic boulders balanced along the hill are decorated.

One must imagine that here and across the hill, the outcrops were once relatively smooth and polished with glacial striations. The subsequent millennia of freezing and thawing weather gradually allowed the cracked surfaces to break up into pieces; and since here at Aral Tolgoi almost all the surfaces are completely exposed to the surrounding atmosphere, surface damage is quite pervasive. By contrast to Baga Oigor, our northernmost complex, here at Aral Tolgoi there are no overhanging slabs or cliffs or protective slopes and draws to shield decorated surfaces from the damage caused by climatic factors.

While there is no way of proving that certain techniques of manual execution can be related to particular chronological periods, a broad overview of several thousand images – as is made possible by the complexes of Aral Tolgoi, Tsagaan Gol, and Baga Oigor – offers strong arguments for a general pattern in the technical development of image making. This has been considered above, but should be expanded here with reference to Aral Tolgoi imagery proper. With

Figure 8 Unfinished aurochs on a glacier-scraped, grooved, and polished surface. Late Pleistocene, Pleistocene–Holocene Transition. Aral Tolgoi. Photo: Gary Tepfer.

only a few exceptions[38], all the images at Aral Tolgoi have been pecked, not engraved, into the rock; and in the vast majority of cases the technique of execution involved direct pecking, where the artist held what must have been a heavy stone in his hand and struck blows directly onto the stone surface. In all these cases there is a consonance of deep and rough pecking, a fundamental directness in the animals' profile, and the frequently vestigial aspect of the animals' legs. These characteristics are apparent in an unfinished image of an aurochs from AT 24 (Fig. 8), executed on a finely polished and grooved surface. In the case of an elk and aurochs from a panel on AT 17 (Fig. 9), one can almost sense the artist striving to control the evenness of his blows and the clarity of the animals' contours.

By contrast, an elk from the same panel as the unfinished aurochs, AT 24, is executed with dense, overall pecking and clear, sharp outlines (Fig. 10). By virtue of its execution and style, this animal can be dated much later, well into the Bronze Age. This much more controlled technique indicates indirect pecking: where the artist held his pecking stone in one hand and his hammer stone in the other. Ultimately this indirect method became the typical manner of rendering imagery in the Bronze Age. It offered control over both the contours and the

---

[38] The exceptions include engraved parts of five archers in a single hunting scene executed in the Bronze Age. See Tseveendorj, Kubarev, Yakobson 2005, p. 169, #65.

Figure 9 Detail of aurochs and elk from a larger hunting scene. Pleistocene–
Holocene Transition. Aral Tolgoi.
Photo: Gary Tepfer.

Figure 10 Elk obscured by lichen. Bronze Age. Aral Tolgoi.
Photo: Gary Tepfer.

interior of the representation, and it allowed for a finely calibrated indication of
texture. As will be seen, the elegant results of that mode of execution are

Figure 11 Unfinished horse. Pleistocene–Holocene Transition. Aral Tolgoi.
Photo: Gary Tepfer.

frequently found in the two large complexes to the north, Tsagaan Gol and Baga
Oigor.

Images on the lowest outcrops on the eastern end of the hill are virtually
illegible, but they appear to be dominated by aurochs, horses, and argali
rendered in a pure contour style. Several equally obscure images of elk are
rendered in a rough silhouette style. As one mounts the hill, there are increasing
numbers of ibex and elk interspersed with aurochs and horses, most executed in
the archaic contoured style. Higher on the hill the same combination of animals
appears, almost always in static, profile postures and even when juxtaposed,
almost always without any physical or psychological relationship with other
animals or figures.

The character of the archaic imagery at Aral Tolgoi – monumental, static,
profile, contoured and highly naturalistic – is beautifully represented by the partial
aurochs from AT 24, at the very top of the hill (Fig. 8). With blunt, rough blows the
artist has evoked the power of the wild animal's neck and chest. Even though also
unfinished, the blackened image of a wild horse from AT 14 conveys the particular
character of that animal's body; its long neck and heavy belly underline a kind of
monumental anonymity in which one image stands in for the animal type.

A large ibex from a deeply eroded and lichen covered surface conveys the
heavy body and large horns of the wild animal despite its almost invisible
appearance (Fig. 7). In the case of an unfinished female elk from AT 19, the

Figure 12 Unfinished female elk. Pleistocene–Holocene Transition. Aral Tolgoi.
Photo: Gary Tepfer.

deeply pecked marks reveal the slightly irregular trajectory of the artist's blows
(Fig. 12). In both the unfinished character of several of these images and the
palpable imprint of the artists' blows, there is conveyed a sense of lost time:
time extended and time interrupted.

The single image of a rhinoceros survives on a small fragment of stone within
the top-most outcrop, AT 22. The animal's horn is lost in a fracture in the stone,
but its heavy body and small, lowered head evoke the power of the beast. Heavy,
even crude, directly pecked marks accentuate the weight of the animal, and the
contrast of its massive body with its vestigial legs adds to the animal's static
monumentality (Fig. 13).

The bull from AT 24, the ibex from AT 21, and the rhino from AT 22 share
with many other images on Aral Tolgoi several characteristics we can, with
certainty, label archaic. These include contours created through rough, deep,
direct pecking; the large, even monumental bodies and, where the animal was
sufficiently finished, the vestigial legs; the static, profile posture; and the lack of
any interaction with other images. There are, however, a number of panels
where animals are overlaid or juxtaposed, but here again there is no indication
of interaction. Each image is its own, individual statement, existing as if in its
own world. An example comes from AT 17 (Fig. 14), where a massive aurochs
was pecked over a horse (here seen across the bull's chest); at some later time,
its tail was over-pecked by a smaller animal in silhouette. We do not understand

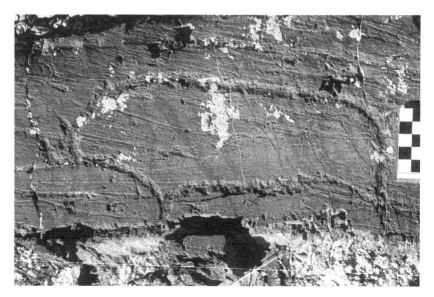

Figure 13 Rhinoceros on a deeply scraped, fragmentary horizontal surface,.
Late Pleistocene. Aral Tolgoi.

Photo: Gary Tepfer.

Figure 14 Aurochs on a deeply scraped horizontal surface, pecked over a horse
and overlaid by an argali. Pleistocene–Holocene Transition. Aral Tolgoi.

Photo: Gary Tepfer.

Figure 15 Elongated elk with vestigial legs, overlaid by an argali. Pleistocene–
Holocene Transition. Aral Tolgoi.

Photo: Gary Tepfer.

the reason for such overlay: there was more than enough room on this rock
surface for all the images to be shown separately, and there is no sense of
intended psychological interaction. Perhaps there existed a conviction that
vitality could be transferred from one image/animal to another, in a kind of
chain of life.[39]

A similar kind of overlay occurs in the case of the elongated elk on AT
16. The large animal measures almost 1.0 m in length. Over its haunch has
been over-pecked a silhouetted argali (Fig. 15). Close by are several other
animals including a horse, a stag, and a later bear; but not one is psycho-
logically related to the others or to the large elk. The elk itself is an
unusually beautiful exemplar of the archaic style: monumental body;
small, fine head; vestigial legs, and its contour created with rough, heavy
blows of a stone. In the elegance and naturalism of its rendering, this elk
deserves comparison with images of elk from the great cave paintings in
France, such as Lascaux.

Across Aral Tolgoi, among what appear to be the oldest images, the basic
motif of image isolation persists. The same rule holds in the case of the oldest
anthropomorphic images on the hill: two figures found at the top of AT 22 on
fractured and gouged fragments of bedrock in the same vicinity as the

---

[39] In later panels from Tsagaan Gol and Baga Oigor, animals are connected in long chains across
a rock panel, while hunters appear at the side. See, for example, *MAIC*: RA_PETR_TG_0913.

Figure 16 Birthing woman on a deeply gouged and fractured surface. Late
Pleistocene. Aral Tolgoi.

Photo: Gary Tepfer.

rhinoceros panel. Their upraised legs and arms identify them as archaic
birthing figures, both executed with rough, direct pecking (Fig. 16).[40]

Scattered over the outcrops are also a few individual anthropomorphic figures
of unknown significance, crude and frontal. Two examples can be seen close to
the ibex on AT 13 (Fig. 7). One tall figure is on the upper center left, the other
(almost illegible) on the far right. The ibex itself has all the characteristics of an
archaic image; at the same time, the naturalism of this animal contrasts with the
crude presentation of the human. This contrast in the definition of anthropomorphic figures (simplistically crude) and animals (impressively naturalistic) is
yet another important and consistent indication of an archaic date. As is the case
in the Paleolithic cave paintings of Europe, it would seem that the most ancient

---

[40] The images are some of the oldest birthing women we have found in our Altai complexes, but
they are not unique. Similarly crude, roughly pecked figures occur in the complexes of Baga
Oigor, Tsagaan Gol, and Khöltsöötiin Gol. They represent an archaic formulation of the primeval
conception of the female as a symbol and source of fertility; but the basic idea recurs in other
forms right down into the Bronze Age, particularly in the complex of Baga Oigor. See Jacobson-
Tepfer 2015, pp. 116–136.

artists at Aral Tolgoi were much more comfortable with the vital representation of animals than they were with that of humans, as if the animals had a more vivid presence. Some might wish to see here an example of hunting magic, in which the artist-hunter represents the animal he seeks for prey, as if to bring it into being. I do not think this is a convincing argument, however. If it were a question of prey and of representing what was being hunted, we would surely find many more small animals of the type that must have been basic sources of meat and fur, such as rabbits, large rodents, foxes and wolves. There must have been another reason for this difference in the representation of animals – always large and impressive animals – and that of humans; but we have yet to understand its source.

The majority of images at Aral Tolgoi, including those that are overlaid, are effectively individual, conceived as singular, static creatures. There are, however, a few panels where we can see the beginnings of what I call a proto-narrative tradition, wherein two elements – a hunter and his prey – are juxtaposed but do not interact. They point to a story to be told, but do not effectively tell it. This device indicates a shifting point of view on the part of the artist: from anonymous chronicler of the animal to active participant in the life of the animal. No longer is the single animal a statement of absolute being; rather, that animal becomes part of a hunt, an object of the artist's externalized action. These scenes thus shift from being objective statements to subjective accounts. Some of these compositions may still be placed within an archaic period: the animals are still contoured with heavy, crude blows, the legs are vestigial, and the invocation of physical and psychological interaction is crude.[41] This early suggestion of a narrative tradition will be important to recall when we consider the rock art of Tsagaan Gol and Baga Oigor. In those complexes we will see a full emergence of a narrative style.

One last example of the introduction of human figures is particularly important because of the nature of the animals represented (Fig. 17). Located on AT 22 – the highest outcrop on the hill and the one containing the most archaic images – this scene is also difficult to decipher within its cracked and abraded surface. Pecked on a horizontal and fragmentary slab, it really needs to be walked around and seen from several different perspectives to be understood. In the image provided here, the forequarters of an inverted horse are visible on the upper left. Another horse appears on the lower edge of the panel, facing to the right. Between the two horses are visible the massive bodies of two ostriches with heavy bodies, long necks, and tiny heads. Between these birds, and seen here on his side, is a frontal figure, his feet to the right. How to read this grouping of images is not clear, but it would seem as if we are looking at a hunter, perhaps, within the context of open steppe, defined by the horses and

---

[41] *MAIC*: RA_PETR_AT_0038.

Figure 17 Two ostriches, two horses, and a central human figure on a fragment
of bedrock. Pleistocene–Holocene Transition. Aral Tolgoi.

Photo: Gary Tepfer.

ostriches. This panel is one of at least three at the top of Aral Tolgoi that include
ostrich-like birds; and in this respect its importance goes beyond introducing the
motif of a hunt.[42] Since ostriches are believed to have disappeared from this part
of Mongolia by the early Holocene (before 9,000 years ago), we can confidently
say that all the ostrich panels date from a period when the climate in this part of
Mongolia was still dry and cold and before the expansion of forests. This panel
thus also indicates that the earliest crude indicators of the proto-narrative
tradition go back to that period.

   Including the birthing figures there are at least 25 anthropomorphic images
that by their postures and the stick-like implements they hold can be dated to the
Early-Middle Holocene, but no later.[43] In addition there are a few human figures
with clearly recognizable large bows.[44] These are among the small number of
images that were done in the Bronze Age. Other later images include several

---

[42] Search *MAIC*: ostrich.   [43] Tseveendorj, Kubarev, Yakobson 2005, p. 202, #1–25.
[44] Ibid., #26–31.

yaks from the late Bronze Age[45] and a rider from the Turkic Period.[46] These few images are concentrated on the lower southwest slope, closest to the plain on which are scattered standing stones, burial mounds, and ritual altars of the Late Bronze–Early Iron Age. Elsewhere in the plain south and west of Aral Tolgoi are many Turkic Period memorial and ritual structures, while further to the west, along the Khara Salagiin Gol, are several lines of burial mounds from the Iron Age.

The imagery on Aral Tolgoi and surface monuments in the surrounding plain intimate a complex tale of the appearance and subsequent disappearance of human communities. If we assume that the making of images indicates the chronology of a human presence, it would seem that hunters and foragers made their way to the west end of Khoton Nuur in the Late Pleistocene and effectively stayed there (most likely on a seasonal basis) through the Early Holocene. At that time the pictorial record effectively ceased at Aral Tolgoi, probably reflecting the closing up of the valley as a result of expanding forests and rising lake levels. To judge from the archaeological evidence around the west end of Khoton Nuur, a significant human presence did not reappear until the late Bronze Age. The very few images from that later period and from the Iron Age, and the nature of the surface monuments south and west of the hill indicate that approximately 3,000 years ago, herders and hunters again began to move seasonally into the region, making their way up the lake basin, west around Aral Tolgoi, and through the Khara Salagiin valley (Fig. 3) to cross the pass into present-day north China.

To judge from the great number of Bronze and Iron Age petroglyphs at Bilüüt 15 km east of Aral Tolgoi, those nomadizing herders may have made camps there on the north edge of Khoton Nuur before moving on to the west. It is interesting to note that the region immediately around Aral Tolgoi encouraged some to erect ritual and even burial monuments but not, apparently, to stay. In fact, there are no good places to establish camps around the base of the hill: the wind coming down from the higher valleys essentially scrubs the treeless plain, while the occasionally flooding Khara Salagiin Gol and Postigiin Gol would have posed regular threats.[47] At the same time, the southern slopes of the lakes are still heavily forested (Fig. 6), a condition that would greatly discourage the herding of small animals. Those slopes have been even more densely forested at the onset of the late Holocene. Lakes and forests would have posed considerable obstacles for herders driving their flocks over the rough moraines on the north shore or along

---

[45] *MAIC*: RA_PETR_AT_0041, RA_PETR_AT_0075, RA_PETR_AT_0078.

[46] Tseveendorj, Kubarev, Yakobson 2005, p. 199, #21.

[47] Signs of deep erosion as a result of flooding and channel change are clearly apparent all along the Khara Salagiin Gol and especially in the immediate vicinity of Aral Tolgoi.

the narrow open shelf on the south shore.[48] Presumably their goal was the much greener valleys on the west side of the ridge, in present-day north China.

The curious millennia-long absence of signs of a human presence on Aral Tolgoi demands an explanation. Within a region that had been so rich in animal life, why did the rock art record come to a close in the Early Holocene just as human actors were making their presence known in rudimentary narratives? And why would the signs of a human presence reappear in the late Bronze Age but then only sparsely, as if passing herders and hunters were few and far between? The answers to these questions lie in the region's paleoenvironment. We know that after the Pleistocene–Holocene transition, forests expanded, pushing back and obliterating what had been open steppe. With that shift in environment disappeared the Pleistocene megafauna, and most particularly the mammoths, rhinoceros, and ostriches. Horses and aurochs, also, were surely pushed out of the heavily forested area, while elk became more abundant. At the same time, we know that lake levels became significantly elevated. This would have made passage around the lakes, between their shores and the heavy forests, virtually impossible for herders of small animals. The route around the large lake now broken into Khoton and Khurgan nuur would have discouraged or even have been impossible for most of those wishing to cross the high ridge to the west. Better routes were definitely to the north in the valleys of the Oigor Gol and its tributaries.

In the case of Aral Tolgoi one may surmise that climate change and the associated transformation of the paleoenvironment were too radical and too rapid to allow for large group adaptation to the new, forested environment. The very character of the region (climate, altitude, and proximity to high mountain ridges) would have limited the choices people could make: hunting and foraging were the most likely means of a livelihood, but agriculture would have been untenable. Herding, also, requiring extensive pasture was not a choice until well into the Bronze Age. Most important, however, was the shift in environment and the resulting precariousness of life at that edge of Mongolia. Until the onset of the Holocene, human survival had depended on hunting and foraging. Those who settled at the west end of Khoton Nuur were, in a sense, trapped: further west the mountain valleys and passes must still have been blocked by glaciers; to the south and north, the high moun-tains, expanding woodlands, and raw moraines were not inviting. To the east, the lake was rising, probably erasing any shoreline for passage. One might

---

[48] These comments are admittedly hypothetical, but they are based on observation of the landscape in the present, when the lake level has radically dropped and the forests have retreated. It is also worth noting that one rarely sees herders with small animals in forested areas: such an environ-ment would simply be too fraught with dangers for sheep and goats: wolves and other predators and the ease of becoming separated from the larger flock and from the herder.

argue that there was no place to go from there except back out to lower elevations along the Khovd or overland north into the Tsagaan Gol basin. But that latter route, which takes one up over the high knot of ridges coming down from Rashanny Ikh Uul, would have been extremely difficult, even treacherous. The heavy forestation around the lake basin and rising lake levels would have deterred any human inhabitation along the lake shores as far as Aral Tolgoi; and these conditions would have persisted until the forests began to retreat and water levels began to drop about 4,500 years ago.

We will see that in the large valleys to the north there was a break in continuity between imagery datable to the early Holocene and the onset of the Bronze Age; such a lacuna points to the relationship of environment and human culture. So, also, at Aral Tolgoi the rhythm of rock art activity should be synchronized with changes in the lake basin's paleoenvironment and the resulting impacts on the ability of humans to maintain an existence there at the edge of the Altai ridge. Herding entered the larger Altai region only after the extensive re-establishment of a steppe/mountain-steppe environment in the late Holocene; but because that steppe environment did not reappear in the region of the Great Lakes until much later, and because the forested environment has maintained itself on the western and southern reaches of the lakes, it may be that herders never penetrated this region in any significant numbers. In this way the pictorial record of Aral Tolgoi came to an end about 7,000 years BP.

4 The Complex of Tsagaan Gol

The Tsagaan Gol complex includes hundreds of surface monuments, primarily from the Bronze and Iron Ages, and thousands of rock-pecked images. The complex is named for the long river extending from Tavan Bogd on the west to Khovd Gol on the east. The satellite image of Tsagaan Gol suggests the rugged character of the landscape here (Fig. 18). On the west, the high, glacier-crested mountains of Tavan Bogd effectively block movement to the west or south. Along the north and south sides of the valley, the slopes are extremely steep and unstable, passable only by ibex. The basic instability of this landscape is, even today, all too evident in the constant rock falls echoing off the steep slopes on the north. This aspect of the Tsagaan Gol landscape must have been even more pronounced in prehistory.

One can divide the river's length and the density of archaeology along it into three sections. The lowest section extends from the river's confluence with Khovd Gol west for about 35 km, to a point where the Khatugiin Gol enters the valley from the southwest. Along this lower section the valley floor is covered with a thin green carpet during the spring and summer months; but within a short distance to the west that green is reduced to narrow strips following

Figure 18 Satellite image of the upper Tsagaan Gol valley. The snow-covered
peaks on the left are those of Tavan Bogd. Just left of center is the sacred
mountain, Shiveet Khairkhan. On the north side of that mountain is the white
stream of Tsagaan Salaa; on the south side of the mountain is the thin, dark
stream of Khar Salaa. In the right half of the image is the combined stream,
Tsagaan Gol. Google Earth.

the braided river and almost lost in an increasingly dry and stony landscape. In
this part of the valley, archaeology is limited to Bronze Age mounds and the
elaborated mounds known as *khirgisuur*[49] on the high terrace over the left bank
and to four-corner Bronze Age burials and Turkic memorial structures tucked
along the base of the slopes. The rock in this section of the river is loose and
crumbly limestone. Only in a few spots, where the stone is a harder greywacke,
have we identified the remains of petroglyphs. The best images are Bronze Age
scenes of caravans making their way up the river to the upper valley.

The middle section of the valley begins at a point marked by the Khatugiin
Gol on the south side of the valley and by the end of a huge moraine filling the
center of the valley like a great stone tongue (Fig. 19). At the upper point of this
section, Bronze Age khirgisuur become more frequent, lining the left bank of
the river and offering a view shed of the moraine, the opening of the Khatugiin
Gol valley, and – upriver – of the sacred mountain Shiveet Khairkhan (Fig. 20).

---

[49] Khirgisuur (khirigsuur) are surface structures that include a central stone mound and a round or
squared stone perimeter. In many cases there are stone rays or paths extending from the central
mound to the external wall, almost always placed in accord with the cardinal directions. In some
parts of Mongolia, khirgisuur have been found to cover simple burials without any grave goods.
Elsewhere there are no found burials. Khirgisuur can range in diameter from as small as five
meters to as large as 100 m or more. Search *MAIC*: khirigsuur.

Figure 19 View over the Tsagaan Gol valley and the central moraine, looking south to the confluence of Khatugiin Gol and Tsagaan Gol.

Photo: Gary Tepfer.

Figure 20 View from the middle Tsagaan Gol west to the black, triangular shape of Shiveet Khairkhan. The khirgisuur in the lower half of the photograph are deliberately built up from white and black stones.

Photo: Gary Tepfer.

That coincidence of monument placement and geography argues that the mounds were intentionally located with reference to their natural environment: that the moraine and the river conferred on that area a particular significance. No less indicative of resonance between the mounds and the river is the way in

Figure 21 View west over the milky flow of Tsagaan Salaa to Tavan Bogd at the border with Russia. In the foreground is an old khirigsuur, partially flooded out. Photo: Gary Tepfer.

which many of the khirgisuur and mounds are constructed with a combination of white and black stones; traditionally the river-worn white stones refer to water and the jagged black stones refer to mountains. As we will see, this duality relates to an important aspect of the upper valley.

This middle section of the river continues to the west, bracketed by lateral moraines crowned by clusters of khirigsuur and burial mounds. The upper point of this section might be considered the tiny administrative settlement (*bag*) of Tsagast Nuur. At this point the valley begins to close in, crowded with a variety of late Bronze Age burial structures. At its western end, the massive shape of Shiveet Khairkhan begins to dominate the landscape. This boat-shaped mountain is revered even today as sacred space.[50] No one but local herders are allowed to climb up to its long, grassy summit, and no one is permitted to hunt the ibex that live there. In fact, except on the western approach, the flanks of the mountain are virtually impassible – steep and very unstable.

The upper section of the valley extends from this point west to the confluence of its two main tributaries, Khar Salaa (the Clear or Black Branch) and Tsagaan Salaa (the Milky or White Branch), and beyond to the ridge of Tavan Bogd. The tributaries are clearly visible in the satellite image. Tsagaan Salaa (on the north) is so named because of the milky coloration derived from its glacial source on Tavan Bogd (Fig. 21). The stream Khar Salaa (on the south) is clear, or "black"; it

---

[50] On the nature of sacred mountains in Mongolia and on their possible history, see Wallace 2016, and Jacobson-Tepfer and Meacham 2016.

Figure 22 View of the Khar Salaa valley from the south flank of Shiveet Khairkhan. The tents in the mid-left indicate the encampment of the author and her team.

Photo: Gary Tepfer.

flows down from springs at the base of Rashaany Ikh Uul (Fig. 22). The two tributaries – the White Branch and the Black Branch – may have established the theme of white and black found first in the khirgisuur of the middle stretch of the river and repeated, regularly, in the stone work of monuments around the sacred mountain, Shiveet Khairkhan. The streams join at the base of Shiveet Khairkhan's eastern flank, forming the white river, Tsagaan Gol.

It is clear that herders and hunters who came up the valley over the last several thousand years have considered the whole landscape to be charged through with reverberations of cosmic order. The massive, glacier-draped ridge on the west, Shiveet Khairkhan in the center, and the varied coloration – white and black – of the two streams suggest the basic formulation of a sacred mandala: with snowy mountains on the edge of the known world, a centrally located sacred mountain, sacred streams from west to east, and a reaffirmation of the four cardinal directions.[51] Maps showing the location of surface monuments and rock art concentrations in the upper valley support this interpretation

---

[51] This argument has been detailed in Jacobson-Tepfer and Meacham 2016. A mandala is, of course, a sacred diagram in Buddhism, best known today through the elaborate formulations of Tibetan Lamaistic Buddhism. Buddhism took root in Mongolia only in the sixteenth century, but it is certainly based in much more ancient shamanic traditions. These, in turn, seem to have emerged from archaic traditions of animism and pantheism. The earliest surface monuments of the Mongolian Altai indicate a deep concern for the significance of directionality and of colors (as in the coloration of stones used in the construction of monuments). For some discussion of these matters, see Jacobson-Tepfer 2015, Chapter 9.

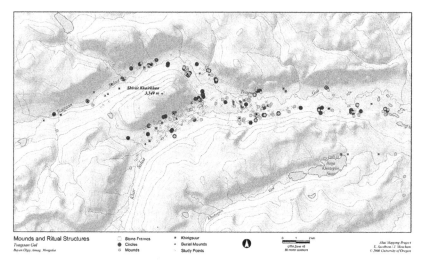

Mounds and Ritual Structures   ☐ Stone Frames   * Khirigsuur
Tsagaan Gol   ● Circles   ▲ Burial Mounds
Bayan Ölgiy Aimag, Mongolia ⊙ Mounds   ∴ Study Points

Figure 23 Map of surface monuments around Shiveet Khairkhan. The
x-marked study points indicate rock art concentrations. Altai Mapping Project.

(Figs. 23). The sacred mountain appears left of center while around it the dense
clusters of study points indicate how cultural remains flank the mountain and
follow the rivers by which it is virtually encircled.

The age of both petroglyphs and surface monuments indicates that the
veneration of Shiveet Khairkhan goes back well into the Bronze Age. In
addition, on a high bridge on the east face of Shiveet Khairkhan, and
seemingly mediating between the valleys of Khar Salaa and Tsagaan Salaa,
stands an elaborate stone altar (*ovoo*) constructed with black and white stones
and taking the form of a cosmic diagram. In the case of this large ovoo, the
central mound of stones, sticks, and flags is built up over what appears to be
a standing stone of the type erected everywhere in the Altai during the Bronze
Age.[52] Extending out from this central mound and pointing in the cardinal
directions are four stone arms in the form of benches as if to accommodate
ceremonial gatherings. This ovoo clearly replicates in miniature form the
cosmic diagram established by Shiveet Khairkhan and the White (Tsagaan)
and Black (Khar) streams. The mountain's sacred character[53] would help to

---

[52] See *MAIC*: VIEW_00012_TG; and see, also, *MAIC*: OVOO_00002_TG for another ovoo, also
    on the slope of Shiveet Khairkhan and overlooking the valley of Tsagaan Gol.

[53] Of course, there is no way of proving that Shiveet Khairkhan has been considered sacred from an
    ancient time; but the coincidence, here, of densely clustered monuments and the diagrammatic aspect
    of geography makes such an interpretation compelling. The sacred character of the mountain is old
    enough to be encoded in its name (Khairkhan). In the present, its ridge is considered to be off-limits to
    any but local inhabitants, and hunting of its wild ibex is strictly forbidden.

explain the unusual density of cultural traces around its base; and the mountain, the east-flowing river, and the river's larger context between the high Tavan Bogd ridge and the Khovd Gol must have reaffirmed the sacred aspect of the valley since the Bronze Age. Ovoo are rooted in a prehistoric belief in the indwelling spirits of the mountains and in the need to acknowledge their power. At the same time, the ovoo mediates between archaic, pre-Buddhist beliefs, Buddhist concepts of sacred space, the larger natural environment, and human existence affirmed in the stone constructions of mounds, ovoo, and standing stones.

The most significant archaeology in the upper Tsagaan Gol is the rock pecked imagery. This material covers bedrock and boulders surrounding the base of the mountain, on either side of Khar Salaa and Tsagaan Salaa, and on the moraine and terraces along the right bank of the upper Tsagaan Gol. Scattered panels can also be found on the high slopes over the river's left and right banks. Across the complex, images occur not just individually; more often they are embedded in densely populated panels that describe herds of animals, or narratives centered on hunting (Fig. 24), herding, or caravanning. Many rock surfaces include large

Figure 24 Scene of archers and fleeing animals on a split boulder. Bronze Age. The clumsy animals above are later additions; the muted bulls below were probably executed later in the Bronze Age. Tsagaan Gol.

Photo: Gary Tepfer.

Figure 25 Unfinished stylized elk under lichen. Late Bronze Age. Tsagaan Gol.
Photo: Gary Tepfer.

numbers of human figures and animals, creating the impression of a human vitality very different from the quiet, unpopulated aspect of the valley today.[54] Scenes of hunting for aurochs, elk, bear, and ibex conjure a region where the valley floor, the steep and unstable side slopes, and the tundra uplands were abundant with wild animals.

The distribution of imagery in the Tsagaan Gol complex reflects ancient patterns of habitation and movement into and through the valley. At several points along the upper valley floor, concentrations of images executed in a similar style point to encampments returned to year after year by a particular group or lineage, as if to reclaim their favored herding grounds. This is apparent in the case of a small hill with several large outcrops on the left bank of the Khar Salaa. The concentration of images, here, of highly stylized elk indicate that this was a favorite encampment for perhaps a lineage or extended family for years during the late Bronze Age (Fig. 25).

A large section of cliff on the south side of Shiveet Khairkhan is so covered with images of Turkic hunters and riders that we dubbed the site "Turkic Cliff." Similarly intermittent concentrations of image types and styles are reflected, also,

---

[54] In the present, the upper Tsagaan Gol supports a small population of Uriankhai and Kazakh herders during the warmer months. In the winter, some retreat to protected winter dwellings, but most return down the valley to the community of Tsengel', on Khovd Gol.

Figure 26 View of a winter dwelling and animal shelter at the base of Shiveet Khairkhan. The long, rocky outcrop protecting the dwelling is covered with Bronze Age rock art.

Photo: Gary Tepfer.

in the rock walls behind present-day winter dwellings (Fig. 26). These are invariably places that are relatively sheltered from the wind that barrels down the valley in the cold months; and they seem to have invited herders back, generation after generation since the Bronze Age. Indeed, in all the high valleys, the distant view of present-day herders' winter dwellings alerted us to where we could find concentrations of ancient rock art: those places that offer protection now did so, also, in antiquity.

Other patterns of image distribution recreate the movement of herders on foot, trudging along the valley or up adjoining slopes. It is useful to imagine the great outcrops of bedrock in the upper valley; they frequently appear to be literal slopes of sandstone of a warm brownish color. In some cases they offer quite intact surfaces, in other cases broken surfaces from which whole chunks of stone seem to be dislodging themselves. Within this context, imagery may suddenly appear in dense concentrations and then just as suddenly disappear, even when the perfection of the empty surface seems to cry out for image making. This strange rhythm in the appearance and disappearance of imagery suggests the trajectories of hunters and herders moving up the valley and over the lower slopes. Where there was good grass for their animals, the sheep and goats would stop to browse or even to rest, and in those places the herders were free to relax and represent in pecked images what they saw in front of their eyes or in their imaginations. To judge from the subjects and styles of the imagery in question, these patterns of movement pertain primarily to the Bronze Age, before Altai herders had adopted horse riding. With the advent of horse dependency by the early Iron Age, that kind of meandering pattern in the distribution of imagery disappears, replaced by a much more episodic distribution. This probably reflects the rhythm of herding on horseback, where the rider was above the ground, watching over larger flocks of animals than had been the case in the Bronze Age.

Given the thousands of images in this complex, it is striking that there are only three or four panels that might be dated to a period earlier than the Bronze Age. An unfinished elk image high on the western base of Shiveet Khairkhan is executed with deep, heavy blows.[55] This manner of execution, the mixed silhouette-contour presentation, and the animal's extreme naturalism indicate a pre-Bronze Age date. A high outcrop on the south side of Shiveet Khairkhan includes images of several different epochs, but a tangle of elk, argali, and possibly an aurochs is distinctively archaic. The images are executed in rough, deep contours and static profiles, and they overlay each other but without any indication of a psychological relationship.[56] Another high outcrop over the left bank of the Tsagaan Salaa, covered with images from the Bronze Age to the Turkic Period, also includes two elk images of a distinctly archaic aspect.[57] At the east end of the complex proper and also on a separate, small hill, are two images of argali or ibex executed with direct, deep blows and now returned to the coloration of the surrounding stone. These could only have been done at an early period (Fig. 27).

The three locations of archaic imagery in the upper complex are distinctive in that they offer a full vantage of the surrounding valley. In that regard, and in the manner in which they are executed, these early images call to mind the work of hunters who may have been looking for their prey in the valley below. Within this earliest group of images, the animals represented are elk, argali, ibex, and aurochs. There are no images of late Pleistocene megafauna nor are there any images of wild horses or bears.

By contrast to these patently pre-Bronze Age images, the rock art we can date to the Bronze Age is impressive not only in its quantity but also in its quality. It literally covers whole outcrops, sometimes suggesting a rock-pecked brocade. There are, of course, many poorly pecked or conceived images; but the extraordinary number of finely conceived and executed panels is almost overwhelming, as if one had wandered into a museum of fine prehistoric art. The images are

---

[55] Jacobson-Tepfer 2019, fig. IV.16.   [56] *MAIC:* RA_PETR_TG_0645.
[57] *MAIC:* RA_PETR_TG_0773.

Figure 27 Fragmented image of an argali on a disintegrating bedrock panel.
Pre-Bronze Age. Tsagaan Gol.

Photo: Gary Tepfer.

typically (but not universally) executed in silhouettes defined by clear outlines and dense internal pecking (Fig. 28). While many images are conceived as individual elements, many are integrated into clear narrative compositions in which there is indicated a beginning (e.g., a hunter), a middle (e.g., fleeing animals), and an implied but never completed end. In most cases the time of these narratives is ongoing, involving action–reaction, but no dénouement. It is striking that within the Bronze Age corpus of imagery in this complex, as well as in the Baga Oigor complex, there are no signs of death: we see animal or human attacks, yes, but no death as a result of those actions.[58]

This veritable museum in the upper Tsagaan Gol did not end with the Bronze Age: the compendium of imagery from the early Iron Age testifies to the extent to which the valley was populated every year by hunters and then by herders seeking good summer pasture for their flocks. The significance of the upper valley in the herders' ritual life continued right into the Turkic Period (mid- to late first millennium CE). That, at least, is what we can presume on the basis of several concentrations of imagery from the Turkic Period and the number of

---

[58] Jacobson-Tepfer 2015, pp. 163–168. There is only one possible representation of a person who has been felled by an attacker, but it is very uncertain that he is dead. See *MAIC*: RA_PETR_TG_0383.

Figure 28 Vertical panel with hunters on the left and a mass of animals
connected by a "life-line." Late Bronze Age. Tsagaan Gol.
Photo: Gary Tepfer.

image stones and memorial altars that cluster around the base of Shiveet
Khairkhan, oriented to the eastward flow of Tsagaan Gol (Fig. 29).

While the broad aspects of the upper valley – excellent pasture, abundant
water, and relatively easy access from the Khovd valley on the east – suggest the
principal ways in which human life was entwined with the natural environment,
another element sheds a sharp light on the creative psychology of the ancient
herders. I have already spoken about their apparent fascination with color. It
shows up in what appears to be the ritual use of white and black stones, or of
river stones (rounded) and mountain stones (jagged), or in the exploitation of
fine red sandstone outcrops (Fig. 30).

It emerges even more clearly when one begins to look carefully at the textures
and coloristic character of the stone and when one notes what appears to be the
deliberate selection by artists of very particular surfaces. In many cases the artist
seems to have sought out a finely polished surface or, as in the case of Figure 30,

Figure 29 Four Turkic image stones and altars at the base of Shiveet Khairkhan. The image stones face east and towards the river (hidden here in the mid-image trough). Tsagaan Gol.

Photo: Gary Tepfer.

Figure 30 Wild horses on a scraped red surface. Bronze Age. Tsagaan Gol.

Photo: Gary Tepfer.

Figure 31 Blue surface with overlaid images from several periods. Tsagaan
Gol.

Photo: Gary Tepfer.

a surface that has been etched by glacial scraping and cracks. In other cases it
was clear that an unusual aspect of the stone drew ancient artists, even over
several hundred years. This is exemplified by a large blue mudstone surface that
preserves in its mineralization the ripples of fine silt of its original location at the
bottom of an inland sea (Fig. 31).

It must be understood that the archaeological wealth of the Tsagaan Gol
valley is extraordinary, even within a part of the world that is rich in petroglyphic imagery and surface monuments beyond what most people would
imagine.[59] The rock art reflects a well-developed and vital narrative tradition,
one that emerged by the early Bronze Age and continued down into the early
modern period. This pictorial tradition almost certainly holds the beginnings of
what would become the great epic tradition of North Asia.[60] It also reflects
a truism that is confirmed by the rock art of Aral Tolgoi, Baga Oigor, and every

---

[59] It is unfortunate that most people, even those with a sophisticated knowledge of world archaeology, are not familiar with the prehistory of North Asia in general and of the Mongolian Altai in
particular. We think of the British Isles and France as extraordinary repositories of ancient art,
and they are. But if one is looking for standing stones, stone memorial structures, and rock art,
the Mongolian Altai is no less remarkable.

[60] I have more extensively discussed the sources of the North Asian narrative tradition and its
reflection in rock art elsewhere; see Jacobson-Tepfer 2015, Chapter 5; and Jacobson-Tepfer
2019, Chapter IX.

other petroglyphic site we have recorded in either the Mongolian or Russian Altai: in this part of the world there was a dedication to naturalistic, pictorial expression, one that lasted at least into the Turkic Period when it appears to have been supplanted by oral recitation as a primary social art form.[61] Throughout that long period (but also continuing down into the present), the valley was visited on an annual basis by an unusual number of people. The quality and quantity of the resulting pictorial material suggests that cultural wealth emerged in concert with the appearance of a critical mass of people who annually brought in and took away narrative and mythic themes. There is no other way to explain both the wealth of material here and at Baga Oigor and the reflections of that material in many adjoining regions. I am arguing, quite simply, that despite the relative emptiness of this valley in the present (and of Baga Oigor to the north), cultural depth seems to have flourished where there was regular human movement and interaction.

But given this pictorial wealth in the Tsagaan Gol valley beginning in the Bronze Age, why are there so few images from an earlier period? Where are the representations of megafauna or even of archaic wild horses? The answers to these questions are embedded within the paleoenvironmental evolution of the valley and the effect of that paleoenvironment on human habitation and culture. In turning to that subject, we have to return to the physical landscape glimpsed in the satellite image of Figure 18.

At a time when aurochs, wooly rhinoceros, *Equus cabellus*, and ostrich were roaming the cold, dry steppe at the western end of present-day Khoton Nuur, the upper Tsagaan Gol valley was certainly choked by ice. The glaciers that had plowed out the river valley eastward for approximately 60 km were receding up the side valleys around Shiveet Khairkhan; but the cold wind that blew off the glaciers and down the Khar Salaa and Tsagaan Salaa valleys would have made this region virtually uninhabitable. Only well into the mid-Holocene (about 8,000 years BP), when scattered groves had appeared in the upper valley offering refuge to animals such as elk and bear, did a few intrepid hunters venture up the Tsagaan Gol to its upper valley. One can imagine that these hunters, drawn by large game – elk, argali, even aurochs – perched themselves on high outcrops from where they could see the animals along the valley floor; and while they lay in wait, scanning the valley for prey, they pecked out their images on the rock surfaces. But the valley was still too inhospitable for regular habitation, and it stayed that way even during the long period of expanding forests and rising lake levels of the middle

---

[61] Of course, oral recitation seems to have emerged at a very early period in the Altai region. This has been commented on by others, for example, Gryaznov 1961, and supported by the apparent exploitation of natural amphitheaters from at least the late Bronze Age. See Jacobson 1994.

Holocene (7,000 to 4,500 years BP). However, long before that process transformed the Tsagaan Gol valley and long before expanding forests had overtaken steppe, hunters had disappeared from the area of Aral Tolgoi, unable to navigate around the huge lake-filled basin, and their hunting for large animals thwarted by heavy forest on the adjoining slopes.

It was only with the onset of the late Holocene, by about 4,500 years BP that hunters and then herders may have begun to move in greater numbers into the upper Tsagaan Gol valley. By then steppe had expanded back into areas that receding glaciers had rendered effectively uninhabitable. Aurochs and wild horses roamed the valley floor while elk and bear had side forests for refuge, open steppe for foraging, and riparian zones for fish, berries, grasses, and forbs. The recession of mountain-top glaciers and snow fields allowed for the return of argali and ibex to the high ridges on either side of the valley and to the long summit of Shiveet Khairkhan. Most important, however, the upper valleys that had been inhospitable for any human occupation became increasingly desirable for summer pasture. Within the mountain zone, the transformation of the economy to one dependent on animal herding seems to have begun to emerge by 4,000 years BP. We can assume that the great period of rock art and surface monuments began in the upper Tsagaan Gol valley during the ensuing period. The resulting flourishing of prehistoric culture in the valley attests to the intertwining of human existence and the natural environment, and the rich store of rock art reflects the ubiquity of stone in this valley: the boulders choking the valley itself and its innumerable terminal and lateral moraines; and the bed rock thrust up along the upper valley floor and side slopes. More than Aral Tolgoi, this valley tells us about stone, its geology and its eons of transformation from volcanic eruptions and the upthrusting of sedimentary layers. The decorating of stone surfaces and the construction of stone monuments here reflect, also, a human fascination with the beauty and possibilities of the material.

Although they lie within the same narrow region of the Mongolian Altai, the valleys of Aral Tolgoi and Tsagaan Gol tell a very different story about the interconnection of the paleoenvironment and human culture. The valley to the north – that of Baga Oigor Gol – tells yet a third story; and in terms of the paleoenvironment that story is the most complex.

5 The Complex of Baga Oigor

Approximately 30 km north of the valley of Tsagaan Gol and beyond the valleys of Ikh Oigor and Dund Oigor is located the valley of Baga Oigor Gol – the Little Oigor River (Fig. 32). Its main source, Shetya Oigor, rises close to the border near Ulaan Davaa – the pass leading over the ridge into Russia's Ukok Plateau.

Figure 32 View of the Baga Oigor valley looking east.
Photo: Gary Tepfer.

From there the river flows east to a point now marked by the tiny settlement of Kök Erik. Just beyond that small clutch of buildings, the river is joined by Tsagaan Salaa[62] flowing in from the north; it then continues to the east for approximately 28 km down to its confluence with Ikh Oigor, the Great Oigor. At that point the river enters a long, narrow canyon, at the end of which it is joined by Khar Yamaa to form the Oigor Gol.

The satellite image of this part of Bayan Ölgiy aimag indicates a mountainous, folded landscape – a veritable mountain-steppe with virtually no tree growth (Fig. 33). This same view also hints at the way in which the Baga Oigor valley is significantly different from that of Tsagaan Gol. We saw that the latter is long, flanked by precipitous slopes, and effectively blocked at its western end by the ridge of Tavan Bogd. This means that the only approaches to the high pastures of the upper valley are from the east or down over precipitous roads from the Ikh Oigor or Khatugiin Gol valleys. By contrast, the valley of Baga Oigor is broad and flanked by slopes that offer relatively easy passage to high pastures for animals and riders. Along its source, the Shetya Oigor, summer pasture is rich

---

[62] This Tsagaan Salaa (White or Milky Branch) should be distinguished from Tsagaan Salaa in the Upper Tsagaan Gol drainage. In Mongolian, physical features of the landscape are frequently named for their colors, sizes, or relationships to adjacent features; thus one finds that names are frequently duplicated. In earlier publications, this complex was referred to as Tsagaan Salaa– Baga Oigor, but it has since been simplified to the name of the larger river.

Figure 33 Satellite image of the Baga Oigor valley. Google Earth.

right up to the pass, and beyond that pass Russia's Ukok Plateau offers abundant pasture and proximity to the forests of eastern Kazakhstan. So, too, the Baga Oigor's tributary Tsagaan Salaa flows down from small streams at the Sailiugem Ridge, beyond which the geography of the Altai Republic's Kosh Agach Region becomes much greener and more forested than on the Mongolian side.

There are several other routes into and out of the Baga Oigor valley; other than in the winter months, these would have been easily negotiated by herders on foot with small and large animals, as well as by horsemen. From the south, one could come over low passes from the Ikh Oigor valley; this route offers a connection down to the Tsagaan Gol valley. Or one could enter from the Khar Yamaa on the northeast through the long, narrow defile visible in the center right of Figure 33. That defile is a particularly important juncture: it is there that the waters of the Oigor rivers are joined into the Oigor Gol, a river that flows sinuously down a broad valley to the Sogoogiin Gol. This river in turn joins Khovd Gol in its flow through the rugged eastern edge of the Altai Mountains and deep into the heartland of western Mongolia. Thus the Baga Oigor is distinguished from the valleys to the south by its relative ease of access from lowlands to the east and from high valleys to the north, south, and west. This geographical accessibility is important to keep in mind. At a time when people had to depend on their own legs and on beasts of burden (yaks, horses, and – later – camels), passes served as significant determinants of cultural transmission and change. Within such a mountainous landscape, rivers were vital and essential routes from one valley to another.

Accessibility and size suggest why there is such a rich array of rock art and surface monuments within the Baga Oigor valley (Fig. 34). These aspects

Figure 34 View across the mouth of Tsagaan Salaa to the slopes of TS II and IV.
In this section, the stone outcrops are extensively covered with petroglyphic
images.

Photo: Gary Tepfer.

also help us understand why it is that here styles and subject matter dating from
the Bronze and early Iron Ages have clear antecedents in the Russian Altai to
the west and in the Sayan Mountains to the north. In fact, it is apparent that from
the beginning of the Bronze Age, the Oigor, Khar Yamaa, and Baga Oigor
valleys were major routes for people moving over the high ridges to seek
pasture and hunting grounds.[63] Within the Baga Oigor complex, the deep age
of that movement is reflected in the surviving rock art record dating back to the
Late Pleistocene and, with one significant break, continuing down into the
Bronze Age, the early Iron Age, and the Turkic Period – a span of at least
11,000 years. In this respect, the valley's archaeological record is significantly
different from that of Aral Tolgoi or Tsagaan Gol. The very depth of prehistory
described by the valley's archaeology testifies, also, to very different paleoenvironmental conditions, especially during the Bronze Age.

   Within the Baga Oigor complex, rock art is distributed across the terraces and
lower slopes along the left bank of the rivers (Figs. 35, 36).[64] The map of its

---

[63] The traces of this transmission are detailed in Jacobson-Tepfer 2015, Chapters 2 and 3.

[64] In this case, the "left bank" refers to the north side of the rivers. Throughout this discussion, the
   side of the river will be referred to as "left" or "right" rather than in reference to compass
   directions.

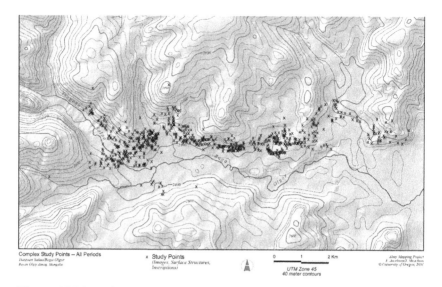

Figure 35 Map of Baga Oigor complex: distribution of concentrations (study points) across the complex. Altai Mapping Project.

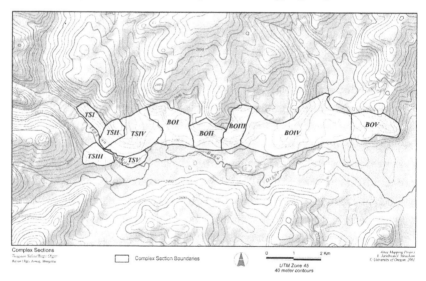

Figure 36 Baga Oigor complex sections. Altai Mapping Project

distribution indicates that imagery is particularly dense at the confluence of Tsagaan Salaa and Baga Oigor, seen also in Figure 34. Similarly, there are dense concentrations along the lower terraces[65] of BO (Baga Oigor) II and BO III.

---

[65] In speaking of a "lower terrace," I refer to the shelf that stretches along the left bank of the river valleys at an elevation of approximately 15 to 45 m above the valley floor.

Figure 37 Scraped boulder with horses, argali, and a human figure. Bronze Age.
Baga Oigor.

Photo: Gary Tepfer.

Rock art is also found on boulders scattered over the uneven land on the right bank of Tsagaan Salaa just before it enters the valley of Baga Oigor. There is a singular lack of imagery in the valley between BO IV and BO V, seen here on the right side of the map; but imagery appears on the slopes above that valley, scattered as if overlooking that lower region. A few concentrations can be found on the lower terraces on the Baga Oigor's right bank. Within the broad valley floor, a few boulders heeled into the ancient glacial till have been decorated (Fig. 37); otherwise the valley floor is quite clear of any decorated surfaces. Unquestionably the distribution of rock art indicated in the map in Figure 35 marks the areas within the valley where hunters and herders had their seasonal dwellings and moved their flocks up the slopes in search of pasture.

The greatest density of imagery dating back to the Late Pleistocene can be found in just a few areas: at the western end of TS I, on the lower terrace; in the lower west section of TS IV and its boundary with TS V; and on the lower terrace at the boundary between BO II and III. These most archaic images include several mammoths,[66] aurochs (Fig. 38), and primitive horses (Fig. 39). These animals are all indicative of a harsh, cold steppe environment such as existed in the late Pleistocene. Their execution – with rough, deeply pecked contours, heavy bodies, and vestigial legs – indicates a very early stage of pictorial imagery. We have recorded one or two archaic elk images within the

---

[66] Search *MAIC*: mammoths.

Figure 38 Aurochs on shattered bedrock. Late Pleistocene. Baga Oigor.
Photo: Gary Tepfer.

Figure 39 Archaic horse. Pleistocene–Holocene Transition. Baga Oigor.
Photo: Gary Tepfer.

Figure 40 Elk, aurochs, and argali on vertical wall. Early Bronze Age. Baga Oigor.

Photo: Gary Tepfer.

complex; they may reflect the existence, even in the late Pleistocene, of sufficient forest cover to support such fauna. As in the case of imagery at Aral Tolgoi, these most archaic images are represented naturalistically; but they are static and unengaged with any other animals. There are no human figures within this group and thus no representations of humans in action.

Within the same general areas in which are found the most archaic images are also a number of panels that are certainly later than those we identify as Pleistocene but do not fall into a clear Bronze Age tradition. These include large, single images of silhouetted or partially silhouetted animals or images of large animals together on one surface but without any significant psychological interaction (Fig. 40). The fauna represented here are predominantly elk, aurochs, and ibex, while mammoths and other megafauna are entirely absent. There are few if any representations of horses within this group of images, and this perhaps reflects the apparent disappearance of the wild horse from this part of North Asia during the Middle Holocene.

Within this representational group, or perhaps slightly later, may be included the earliest images of hunters. These figures are large, usually frontal, and hold weapons reminiscent of clubs or an unusual kind of bow (Fig. 41). They may be juxtaposed with animals; but between hunter and animal there is no sense of a psychological connection. On the other hand, as crude as these hunters are, they represent the earliest indications of a narrative tradition – one that will

Figure 41 Hunter, ibex, and two birthing women. Pre-Bronze Age (the birthing
women) and Early Bronze Age (hunter and large ibex). Baga Oigor.
Photo: Gary Tepfer.

come to dominate the rock art of this complex just as it came to dominate the
Tsagaan Gol complex. Within the grouping in Figure 41, the basic story is
inferred by the crude frontal hunter juxtaposed with the large ibex above. In
addition there are two faintly visible birthing figures, one in center-right and the
other almost lost under orange lichen. It would seem that the individual who
pecked out the hunting scene on this boulder deliberately laid it over the birthing
women executed at an earlier period. From all that we have been able to learn
about the most ancient images of females in this rock art, the birthing woman
was the probable sign of the regeneration of life.[67] Thus this proto-narrative
functions through the juxtaposition of images rather than through their actual
interaction. In the process, it introduces into the basic tale signs of a deeper time.

The vast majority of decorated panels in the Baga Oigor valley can be dated
to the Bronze Age; generally these reflect the subjects and styles found at
Tsagaan Gol but with several additional elements. One unusual motif is

---

[67] Jacobson-Tepfer 2015, Chapters 2–6, *passim*.

Figure 42 Bell-shaped figure with elk and aurochs. Bronze Age. Baga Oigor. Photo: Gary Tepfer.

a frontal, faceless figure with bell-shaped outer body and horns. This figure type does not occur in the Tsagaan Gol complex nor does it appear at Aral Tolgoi. The example shown here (Fig. 42) is juxtaposed with a female elk and an aurochs in which appears the image of another animal. These elements together suggest the female character of the strange image, her association with female animals and the function of birthing. This is even more explicit in the large figure of a horned and faceless being, located frontally on a boulder overlooking the confluence of the Tsagaan Salaa and Baga Oigor. In this case the figure is clearly giving birth, and animals approach her from the side as if to reaffirm the fact of her fecundity.[68] Many of these images are located along the riverbank or facing out to the river, the south, and the snow-covered ridge of Taldagiin Ikh Uul. This strange, bell-shaped figure is one of the image types at Baga Oigor that point to a connection with an early Bronze Age culture in Russian Altai (the

---

[68] See *MAIC*: PETR_00256_OI, PETR_00257_OI. For more images of this figure type at Baga Oigor, see *MAIC:* Spirit Figures.

Figure 43 Elk. Bronze Age. Baga Oigor.

Photo: Gary Tepfer.

Karakol Culture) and, further to the north, with a culture in the upper Yenisei drainage.[69]

More typical of Bronze Age imagery at Baga Oigor are animals and human figures almost always executed in a careful, silhouette style. Many are individual representations, such as the case of a fine elk on a low boulder in TS IV (Fig. 43). Many decorated panels involve complex scenes including several figures arranged in such a manner that their focused action implies extended space and time. This is visible in a scene where several figures with weapons surround a small bear (Fig. 44). The bows, cudgels, and spears that the figures hold indicate a date in the middle Bronze Age; and the manner in which the figures surround the bear conspires to create the impression of our movement, also, around that center from below to above. Figures rushing in from the right and left further extend the time and space of the narrative in a manner one could almost call sophisticated.[70]

In contrast to the static character of archaic imagery, the animals and humans in rock art of the Bronze Age frequently express considerable vitality – even

---

[69] See Jacobson-Tepfer 2015, Chapter 3. A number of images of the same type have been found in a poorly excavated site along the Godon Gol, close to the confluence of that river with the upper Khovd (Kovalev 2015).

[70] For a more developed discussion of this panel, see Jacobson-Tepfer 2019, pp. 118–121.

Figure 44 Bear surrounded by hunters. Bronze Age. Baga Oigor.
Photo: Gary Tepfer.

a delight in the representation of movement and interaction, both physical and psychological. Many of these panels represent hunting scenes or scenes of animals together, as well as scenes of family caravans centered on heavily loaded yaks as beasts of burden. Large panels including humans, animals and birds recreate a world of hunting or herding. In Figure 45, for example, we are in the space of several hunters surrounded by rushing, leaping animals, while the upper part of the rock is marked by great spread-winged birds that we see as if from above. As at Tsagaan Gol, there are images of conflict between individuals or groups of figures; but these are relatively unusual and appear to reflect conflict over hunting grounds or pasture land rather than any large group combat. With this material one confronts the full development of a narrative expression that sometimes combines spatial perspectives or continues over two or more surfaces, as if to extend the sense of time. These narrative devices are visible in Figure 45, where the scene takes place across a rough outcrop that actually extends further than is here visible in the photograph. The hunters and animals create the extension of space on earth, while the birds above pull our imagination into a higher realm.

When we speak here of the Bronze Age we are referring to a tradition that lasted for at least 1,000–1,200 years. Within that long span of time, faunal types indicate what must have been changing environmental conditions. It seems that

Figure 45 Hunters, wild animals, and birds. Bronze Age. Baga Oigor.
Photo: Gary Tepfer.

during the early Bronze Age, images of aurochs disappeared, replaced by yaks both wild and domesticated. Argali were infrequently represented, but images of elk and ibex became important within hunting scenes. The elk images indicate that forests that had expanded in the Middle Holocene were still extensive enough to support that animal, while grassy upper slopes supported the wild ibex population.

Only during the latter half of the Bronze Age do we find representations of moose (*Alces alces*) at Baga Oigor, but these are uniquely found in the area described by TS I, II, III, and IV, and almost always close to the river. Dependent on the riparian browse of willows, shrubs, and water grasses, moose representations imply an environment considerably wetter and more forested than exists today.[71] The appearance of several moose representations in that area at the confluence of Tsagaan Salaa and Baga Oigor suggests the nature of habitat at a much earlier period; today, as can be seen in Figure 34, the landscape is completely treeless. Similarly, and with one important exception (Fig. 48), there are few panels from the Bronze Age in which bear are

---

[71] Search *MAIC*: moose; and see, in particular, RA_PETR_OI_0048. Neither in the Baga Oigor valley nor in any other valley of this part of Bayan Ölgiy does there still exist the riparian habitat in association with forest cover that could support moose.

Figure 46 Rider and animals. Early Iron Age. Baga Oigor.
Photo: Gary Tepfer.

represented. This kind of pictorial absence could refer to the absence of the animal from the habitat; but it could, of course, also refer to a lack of interest in representing that animal, for whatever reason.[72] The appearance of Bronze Age imagery across and higher on the slopes over the rivers indicates a growing population of seasonal inhabitants and a greater use of the slopes for the pasturing of animals.

Scattered across the complex are single images and compositions that by style and subject matter can be dated to the late Bronze and early Iron Ages. The diagnostic elements here include the representation of riders and animals rendered with a particular form of stylization (Fig. 46).[73] There are also images and several inscriptions that can be dated to the Turkic Period; but these are significantly fewer in number than what we find at Tsagaan Gol.

[72] Throughout the history of Altai rock art, some animals were regularly represented while others were never or rarely represented. There are certainly several reasons for that discrepancy, including economic importance (or lack thereof), physical impressiveness (e.g., argali are more impressive than marmots), and the animal's significance within a mythic setting.

[73] For a discussion of these changes at the end of the Bronze Age, see Jacobson-Tepfer 2019, Chapter XI.

This brief overview of the imagery in the Baga Oigor complex indicates a rather different pattern than what we have found in the case of the other complexes. At Aral Tolgoi, rock art simply ended during the Early Holocene – well before any signs of a Bronze Age. At Tsagaan Gol, by contrast, and with only a few isolated exceptions, the pictorial record didn't begin until the Bronze Age and then it was continuous right through into the Turkic Period. But in the Baga Oigor complex, while there are images that insist on a human presence in the valley already in the Late Pleistocene, there is a curious break – a lacuna – between the most archaic images and the beginnings of the Bronze Age. The question becomes how to explain that strange break, an interval that must have lasted several thousand years.

As in the complexes already considered, the answer to this question lies within the landscape's indications of ancient geological change. These include not only the ubiquitous signs of glacial movement over boulders and bedrock – leaving behind scrape, stutter, and the fracturing of stone – but also signs of more cataclysmic events within a few large areas. These are visible in the satellite image of the valley seen in Figure 33. The first is an area extending from a high point west of the large lake in the Tsagaan Salaa valley down to the point where Tsagaan Salaa enters the Baga Oigor valley (Fig. 47). The second

Figure 47 Satellite image of the Tsagaan Salaa valley and the upper Baga Oigor valley. Google Earth.

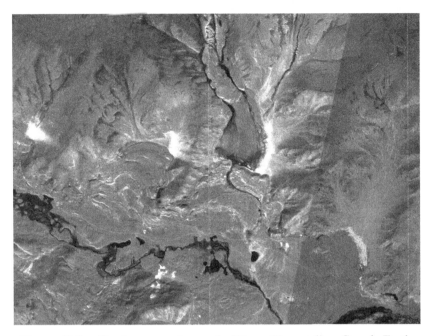

Figure 48 Satellite image: eastern end of Baga Oigor valley. Google Earth.

area includes the main valley itself but most particularly that section located parallel to the south side of TS IV and BO I. It is visible in the lower right third of Fig. 47. The third area includes a large section on the east end of the valley (Fig. 48). This area is dominated, in its upper half, by a spade-shaped formation fed by two streams and, below that, by a large uneven section through which flows a small stream south into the larger Baga Oigor. The events traced in these sections of the physical landscape reveal the probable cause of the hiatus in Baga Oigor's rock art between the late Pleistocene and the early Bronze Age.

Within the first area (Fig. 47) – that of the Tsagaan Salaa valley – the trajectory of ancient glacial action is clearly visible in the scraped side walls on the left bank of the stream. Although the angle of the image obscures the right bank of the stream, the steep slope on that side of the river also retains traces of the movement of an ancient valley glacier. A larger view of this section of the complex, including the tributary streams on the northwest of the large pond, clarifies how ancient glaciers descended from three valleys and converged in the corridor now described by the Tsagaan Salaa. In this section of the Tsagaan Salaa valley, the slope over the left bank is covered with rock art from the Bronze Age. Lower down are earlier images, including some of the most archaic images in this valley. These are located on a terrace approximately

58 m above the present-day valley floor. Pecked into cracked and often tumbled boulders, these include images of naturalistic but static aurochs and elk.

The same satellite image indicates that the valley basin was once filled with a large lake, certainly left in the wake of the retreating valley glacier. What remains today of that lake is a pond connected by a stream to a smaller body of water; this in turn drains into the marshy area at the mouth of the Baga Oigor valley. In this area at the mouth of Tsagaan Salaa the land is hummocky, as if formed from the debris of ancient glacial till. In the present, this hummocky area is covered with rough grass and large, scattered boulders, spread helter-skelter over the land.

The second area to be considered lies on both sides of Baga Oigor as it runs parallel to TS IV and BO I. In the satellite image of Fig. 47, there are many signs of the ancient surge of water over the landscape. They appear in the lineation of the surface as if shaped by currents over a long period of time; they are also revealed in the sharp edge of a kind of medial moraine on the north side of the river. Perhaps the most vivid signs of heavy water flowing over an extended period are indicated by boulders in that area. In one case, a boulder with the image of an early Bronze Age elk was found buried in silt.[74] In several other cases – all located within the flat plain of TS V – boulders bear the signs of having been water-worn: smoothed and polished as if by the movement of flowing water over a long period of time. In the most startling example, a large rough boulder with archaic images of a heavy horse and a massive bear was apparently torn up from its original site higher on the Tsagaan Salaa and tumbled to where it now rests, inverted, on the north side of TS V.[75] In subject and in style, the two images point back to the Late Pleistocene. Clearly this boulder must have been wrenched from its original setting and transported here in a major flooding event. In other words, this second area within the complex reveals many signs of a massive deluge out from the valley of Tsagaan Salaa at some point after the Late Pleistocene and well before the Bronze Age.

The third area for consideration is located on the eastern end of the valley (Fig. 48). Here the river forms channels between marshy areas before flowing into a joined stream that will pass through the long, narrow defile into the larger Oigor Gol valley. In this third section, the valley floor alternates between large smooth areas and others that can only be described as the fossilized remnants of an ancient flow of glacial debris carried by tides of fast-moving water. A similar situation is evident in the upper half of this section where a spade-shaped formation terminates at a dam formed by a great moraine. The rivers flowing into this curious trench trace the path of a long-disappeared glacier that plowed

---

[74] *MAIC*: RA_PETR_OI_0492, RA_PETR_OI_0493.   [75] Jacobson-Tepfer 2019, pp. 62–65.

down from the higher mountain ridge and pushed up the massive terminal moraine. But the land also reveals the cataclysmic force that appeared when the dam was breached in its center and poured out of the high reservoir, carrying massive amounts of debris below to the west and east. The result is easily visible in the satellite image. What remains of that event today is only the disarranged landscape, a small amount of water accumulating behind the breached moraine, and a small outflow that makes its way down into Baga Oigor Gol. It is striking that in this area of the complex, between BO IV and V, there are very few images and those that do exist appear to be either Late Bronze or Early Iron Age in date. On the other hand, ceremonial altars of a Bronze Age date are found across the east-facing slope and the higher ridge of BO IV; in addition, small stone altars have been constructed across the remaining terrace of the breached moraine. While these altars seem to be recent in date, they may well reflect a kind of cultural memory and the re-consecration of much more ancient ritual structures. Such a pattern of re-consecration is ubiquitously indicated in the ovoo, those stone mounds on ridges and at passes to which travelers have been adding stones and sacred relics for thousands of years.[76]

There are many more signs of dramatic reformation of the valley, both on a microscopic level (e.g., glacial scrape, shattered bedrock) and on the larger, macroscopic level we have just considered. At the same time, there are recurring signs that over thousands of years, humans have responded to the changes in the valley either directly or in the form of cultural memory through the addition of stones to ovoo or to altars. The awareness of change – even change in the distant past – is embedded, also, in the strange image of a winged, horned, and faceless being, repeated across the upper valley and almost always facing the river and the south (Fig. 42). At the least, this image, like that of the occasional horned masks in the valley, appears to refer to a supra-human realm – the realm of spirits and ancestors; there are also strong indications that it reflects an ancient concern with regeneration.[77] A deep if unconscious awareness of geological change may also be visible in the manner in which hunters and herders selected for their pictorial records stones marked by the passing of glaciers and organized their compositions in order to exploit those signs.[78]

This brings us back to the question raised earlier in this section: how can we account for the curious lacuna in rock art of the Baga Oigor complex: a break that seems to have extended from the Pleistocene–Holocene transition down to

---

[76] A large ovoo at the base of Shiveet Khairkhan, in the Tsagaan Gol valley, was mentioned earlier.
[77] Jacobson-Tepfer 2010, pp. 102–113.
[78] For a fuller discussion of this point with reference to the Baga Oigor valley in particular, see Jacobson-Tepfer 2019, pp. 50–66.

just before the onset of the Late Holocene? What aspects of the history of human occupation of the valley were shaped by the geology and climate of that long period? It seems certain that at a time when the landscape was still best described as a cold mountain-steppe with scattered forest refuges, the only humans that came into the valley were in search of large game. They made their camps along the terraces just over the river valley; and from that vantage they could see the aurochs, wild horses, and mammoths that had drawn them to the broad basin. At that time the glaciers that had filled the Tsagaan Salaa valley and those that still overlay the mountaintops were in retreat, leaving behind lakes impounded by terminal moraines and a virtual sea of glacial till. It seems as if the area at the mouth of Tsagaan Salaa, before it entered the Baga Oigor valley, was considered particularly propitious for hunting, as was the terrace along BO II-III.

Over hundreds of years, the dry steppe character of the land was overtaken by more moisture tolerant vegetation. Forests spread over the slopes above the valley, the variety of fauna changed, and the boulders and bedrock that would be exposed in the Late Holocene became covered by thick vegetation – the kind that still covers the north side of Aral Tolgoi. To judge from decorated boulders at the mouth of Tsagaan Salaa and those worn and tumbled in the plain of TS V, at some time late in the mid-Holocene, the lake filling the valley of Tsagaan Salaa broke through its dam and flooded down into the larger valley, carrying with it huge amounts of glacial till as well as boulders both decorated and undecorated. That flooding continued for some time, transporting with it the stones and silt that would be deposited in great, fossilized currents and ultimately frozen in place by rough vegetation. Further down the valley, the much larger lake above BO IV and V also broke through its terminal moraine and washed what must have been thousands of tons of earth and rock in one large stream into the Baga Oigor valley. Of course, we cannot know for certain if these two flooding events occurred at approximately the same time, but it is probable that they did, that they reflect the point at which the moraines built up by glaciers failed behind the weight of the water they had impounded; or perhaps the breaking of the dams reflects seismic events such as still occur regularly in this part of Mongolia.

At some point after these cataclysmic changes in the valley, when the floods had receded and the churned earth settled into fossilized ridges, people began again to trickle into the Baga Oigor basin and to again place their temporary camps on the terraces over the valley floor. As in an earlier period, they were certainly hunters and foragers. By the inception of the late Holocene, about 4,500 years BP, the land had become more hospitable, first to hunters and then, much later, to herders. This gradual but decisive change marked the inception of the great rock art tradition of the Bronze Age.

The chronology of rock art at the three complexes of Aral Tolgoi, Tsagaan Gol, and Baga Oigor indicates significant variations in the relationship between the paleoenvironment and human habitation and culture. At the same time, the rock art raises the issue of shared populations in prehistory: that is, the extent to which rock art imagery reflects the movement of people from one valley to another. This is a far larger topic than can be discussed here; but the very proximity of the three complexes requires some comment.

The complex of Tsagaan Gol lies approximately 45 km north of Aral Tolgoi. That relatively small distance belies the rugged landscape between the two valleys including the massif of Rashaany Ikh Uul (3,368 m) and the knot of highlands and peaks extending off Tavan Bogd. Whether on foot, as in early prehistory, or since the late Bronze Age by horse or camel, to travel from Aral Tolgoi to the Tsagaan Gol valley, one would have to thread ones way north, following rivers and streams coming down from Rashaany Ikh Uul until one reached the mountain itself (Fig. 49). From there the traveler might traverse a mountainous highland northeast into the valley of Khatugiin Gol and, thence down into the middle Tsagaan Gol valley. Alternatively, the challenge would be to cross the Rashaany Ikh Uul's glaciated north-facing flank and descend into the valley of Khar Salaa. That small stream now flows through a treacherous tundra-like section into a more open valley on the south side of the mountain

Figure 49 View over the high plateau of Rashaan Gol as it flows down into the basin of Aral Tolgoi on the south.

Photo: Gary Tepfer.

Shiveet Khairkhan. While this overland trajectory is well known in the present day – regularly used, even, by tourists doing camel and horse trekking into the Tavan Bogd region – in an earlier day it would certainly have been very challenging. Up into the late Bronze Age, long glacial tongues would have blocked any movement over Rashaany Ikh Uul, and heavy snow would have made the overland trek into the Khatugiin Gol valley treacherous. In effect, in prehistory the passage north from Aral Tolgoi would have been possible only by descending down the lakes to the valley of the largest river, Khovd Gol, and following that river north to its confluence with Tsagaan Gol.[79]

By contrast, the route out of the Tsagaan Gol valley north to the Baga Oigor valley would have been relatively feasible either on foot or on horseback. It would require wending ones way up the small stream called Tydyg (on the north side of Tsagaan Salaa opposite Shiveet Khairkhan) into the Ikh Oigor valley; or by following a rough slope up into the same valley from a point east of the *bag* center Tsagast Nuur. From the valley of Ikh Oigor the route to Baga Oigor over two more passes would have been relatively easy. This argues for the regular passage of herders out of Baga Oigor and down to Tsagaan Gol, and the reverse. In addition, there are clear indications that during the Bronze Age, herders and hunters moved from present-day Russian Altai and the Sayan mountain region into northwestern Mongolia.[80]

6 Rock Art and the Anatomy of Deep Time

It is traditional for any study of rock art to refer to the natural context within which the site or complex is found and to give the reader a sense of the surrounding landscape. In some cases, the researcher even attempts to explain that landscape as it was, contemporary with the rock art's execution; more rarely, a researcher will explore in detail the way in which subject, style, and the paleoenvironment were inextricably linked. In the preceding discussion I have tried to take this last approach, but to pursue its implications further by comparing the fates of three major rock art complexes in the Mongolian Altai. By examining the changing geology and climate of a mountainous region, I have tried to demonstrate how the study of this pictorial record – its subjects, styles, cultural significance, and dating – can only be understood within a natural world considered in flux. Each of the complexes we have addressed presents very different facts relating to their past – facts driven by glacial action, climate change, and the resulting shifts in vegetation and faunal regimes.

---

[79] Using Bronze Age imagery, it is possible to trace a route from Bilüüt, on the north shore of Khoton Nuur, down to the Khovd, down the Khargantyn Gol, to Tsagaan Gol.

[80] Jacobson-Tepfer 2019, pp. 182–202.

Without sustained reference to that larger context, the lack of symmetry between the three complexes could be simply ignored or dismissed as yet one more curious aspect of deep time.

Earlier I referred to the paleoenvironment as the macrocosm of time, and human expressive and social change as the microcosm. This is particularly true in a region where for thousands of years humans have faced their natural world without any protective barriers: no major buildings to shield them from the elements, no urban infrastructure, no state organization. As a result, the paleoenvironment and human response to it may be considered as two cogs within a well-calibrated precision instrument, where even the slightest changes in the former can catalyze changes in the latter. Considered from this perspective, the study of rock art is incomplete without situating it firmly within a natural world understood as shifting in all its parts, as if it were an organic whole.

There is a particular aspect of rock art that sums up the interconnection between environment and human creativity and merits attention here. The following comments could most certainly apply to all petroglyphic rock art, but now I am only concerned with the pictorial record of Aral Tolgoi, Tsagaan Gol, and Baga Oigor. That aspect is the rock itself on which the images are pecked or engraved. I have already spoken about the petrology of the valleys and of how the patina of both the stone surface and the pecked image is dependent on many interconnected aspects: of the stone itself and of the ambient environment, within the passing of time. Indeed, in the case of the pecked image, that slow shift in coloration from light to dark over a period of thousands of years is a measure of deep time and of the environmental changes carried with it.

Yet another critical aspect of that stone impacts the human traces on it. It is well represented by an image from the Tsagaan Gol complex (Fig. 50). At the eastern base of Shiveet Khairkhan, on a massive stone outcrop, an unknown artist in the late Bronze Age pecked out a fine ibex on a vertical surface. In his rendition, the artist captured the powerful grace of the wild animal, the size of its horn, and the ease with which the caprid carries that weight. Its front legs have been almost completely lost, but its hind legs indicate that the animal was meant to be seen in motion. Just as its posture indicates change in space (and thus in time), so the caprid's patina indicates process: we see the ibex as its coat seems to slide from a dirty light gray to a rich brown. In other words, the image takes us back to that point in time, about 3,000 years ago, when the original white of the crushed surface had begun to darken and shift to a color that would help to indicate its Bronze Age date.

However, change in patina is hardly the only process visible here. The deep brown gouge in front of the ibex and the scrape and stutter visible above the animal testify to the ancient passing of glaciers and their crushing up against the

Figure 50 Caprid. Late Bronze Age. Tsagaan Gol.
Photo: Gary Tepfer.

mountain's rock wall. The difference between the rich and varied hue of the
stone surface and the dead gray of the stone matrix also measures the slow
interaction of the stone's mineral character, ambient humidity, surface bacterial
growth, and dust falling on the basic stone, and leading over thousands of years
to the lovely, warm-colored patina and the almost lacquer-like surface texture.
Those changes are not all, of course. Before our eyes the stone itself is disintegrating, its hardened surface spalling and whole chunks of matter breaking
from the matrix. Finally, to add to that process of dissolution, lichen has taken
root in cracks and crevices; it will continue to spread, weakening the surface and
adding to the breakdown of the stone.

What we see here so decisively is the process of stone's inevitable dissolution, the eons-long disintegration of hard bedrock. Of course, the stone itself had
already gone through a long process of coming-into-being: from its earliest
form as sediment to its maturity as solid stone and now to what one can only
think of as its old age, its slow coming apart and return to an ultimate state of
pebbled matter. Within this transformation, lasting over thousands – no, millions – of years, the lovely caprid has taken its place, moving for an eternity
across its slowly disappearing world.

All stone art in the open-air ages and acquires the patina of time. Sculptures darken and the stones in architectural settings may disintegrate. In most cases, however, those changes are attended to and can be arrested, perhaps replaced with new stones. Even in the case of structures destroyed by war or neglect, the original is often recreated in some meaningful form. This kind of protection and renewal is not possible with prehistoric rock art. The ibex at the base of Shiveet Khairkhan is disintegrating, and that change cannot be reversed. The image and its surrounding space serve as a measure of the way in which the paleoenvironment impacts and shapes human creativity and our reception of it. An observer might quickly object that the artist of this ibex never even imagined what would happen to his little animal or to the surface on which it was pecked; and that, therefore, to speak of the changes in the rock surface as a part of the expressive force of the image is ridiculous. But the nature of rock art here or anywhere is that it is in and of its natural world, it cannot be extracted from its stone context and ambient climate. However much we might wish to ignore those changes that were not anticipated by the original artist, as sentient beings we are drawn by the signs of deep time. For complex reasons an object or an image acquires added luster from having survived time and the elements; however changed, the image becomes more moving. In this manner, the small ibex becomes a measure of deep time, a microcosmic exposition of its anatomy of change.

References

Barton, L., P. J. Brantingham, and J. Duxue. 2007. Late Pleistocene Climate Change and Palaeolithic Cultural Evolution in Northern China: Implications from the Last Glacial Maximum. In: Madsen, D. B., Chen, F.-H., and Xing, G. (Eds.), *Late Quaternary Climate Change and Human Adaptation in Arid China*. Elsevier, Amsterdam, pp. 105–128.

Bednarik, Robert. 2001. *Rock Art Science: The Scientific Study of Palaeoart*. Brepols Publishers, Belgium.

Blomdin, Robert, J. Heyman, A. P. Stroeven, et al. 2014. Glacial Geomorphology of the Altai and Western Sayan Mountains, Central Asia. *Journal of Maps* 12: 123–136.

Blyakharchuyk. T. A., H. E. Wright, P. S. Borodavko, W. O. van der Knaap, and V. Ammann. 2004. Late Glacial and Holocene Vegetational Changes on the Ulagan High-Mountain Plateau, Altai Mountains, Southern Siberia. *Palaeogeography, Palaeoclimatology, Palaeoecology* 209: 259–279.

Blyakharchuyk. T. A., H. E. Wright, P. S. Borodavko, W. O. van der Knaap, and V. Ammann. 2007. Late Glacial and Holocene Vegetational History of the Altai Mountains (Southwestern Tuva Republic, Siberia). *Palaeogeography, Palaeoclimatology, Palaeoecology* 245: 518–534.

Deng, T. 2006. The Fossils of the Przewalski's Horse and the Climatic Variation of the Late Pleistocene of China. In: Maskour, M. (Ed.), *Equids in Time and Space* (Proceedings of the 9th Icaz Conference). Oxbow Books, Oxford, pp. 12–19.

Derevianko, Anatoly P., W. Roger Powers, and Demitri B. Shimkin, eds. 1998. *The Paleolithic of Siberia*. IAE-Siberian Division, Russian Academy of Sciences, Novosibirsk; University of Illinois Press, Urbana and Chicago.

Foronova, Irina V. 2006. Late Quaternary Equids (Genus *Equus*) of South-Western and South-Central Siberia. In: Mashkour, Marjan (Ed.), *Equids in Time and Space*. Oxbow Books, Oxford, pp. 20–30.

Gaunitz, Charleen, Antoine Fages, Kristian Hanghøj, et al. 2018. Ancient Genomes Revisit the Ancestry of Domestic and Przewalski's Horses. *Science* 360: 111–114.

Gibbon, Guy. 2017. The Science of Rock Art Research. In: David, Bruno, and McNiven, Ian J. (Eds.), *The Oxford Handbook of the Archaeology and Anthropology of Rock Art*. Oxford Handbooks Online, Oxford, 24 pp.

Goebel, Ted. 1999. Pleistocene Human Colonization of Siberia and Peopling of the Americas: An Ecological Approach. *Evolutionary Anthropology* 8, 6: 208–227.

Grunert, Jörg, Frank Lehmkuhl, and Michael Walther. 2000. Paleoclimatic Evolution of the Uvs Nuur Basin and Adjacent Areas (Western Mongolia). *Quaternary International* 65/66: 171–192.

Gryaznov, M. P. 1961. Drevneyshiye pamyatniki geroicheskogo eposa yuzhnoy Sibiri. *Arkheologicheskii Spornik* 3: 7–31.

Gunin, P. D., E. A. Vostokova, N. I. Dorofeyuk, P. E. Tarasov, and C. C. Black. 1999. *Vegetation Dynamics of Mongolia*. Kluwer Academic Publishers, Dordrecht.

Guthrie, R. D. 2001. Origin and Causes of the Mammoth Steppe: A Story of Cloud Cover, Woolly Mammal Tooth Pits, Buckles, and Inside-Out Beringia. *Quaternary Science Reviews* 20: 549–574.

Helskog, Knut. 2014. *Communicating with the World of Beings*. Oxbow Books, Oxford.

Herren, Pierre-Alain, Anja Eichler, Horst Machguth, et al. 2013. The Onset of Neoglaciation 6000 Years Ago in Western Mongolia Revealed by an Ice Core from Tsambagarav Mountain Range. *Quaternary Science Reviews* 69: 59–68.

Herzshuh, Ulrike. 2005. Palaeo-moisture Evolution in Monsoonal Central Asia during the last 50,000 Years. *Quaternary Science Reviews* 25, 163–178.

Jacobson, E. 1993. *The Deer Goddess of Ancient Siberia. A Study in the Ecology of Belief*. E. J. Brill, Leiden.

Jacobson, E. 1994. Turu-Alty (Analysis of a Siberian 'Sanctuary') (with V. D. Kubarev). *Altaica* 1994, 4: 18–29.

Jacobson, E., V. D. Kubarev, and D. Tseveendorj. 2001. *Mongolie du Nord-Ouest: Tsagaan Salaa/Baga Oigor*. Répertoire des Pétroglyphes d'Asie central, Fascicule no. 6. 2 vols. De Boccard, Paris.

Jacobson-Tepfer, E. 2015. *The Hunter, the Stag, and the Mother of Animals*. Oxford University Press, Oxford.

Jacobson-Tepfer, E. 2019. *The Life of Two Valleys in the Bronze Age: Rock Art in the Mongolian Altai*. Eugene, Oregon: Luminaire Press.

Jacobson-Tepfer, E., V. D. Kubarev, and D. Tseveendorj. 2006. *Mongolie du Nord-Ourest. Haut Tsagaan Gol*. Répertoire des Pétroglyphes d'Asie central, Fascicule no. 7. 2 vols. De Boccard, Paris.

Jacobson-Tepfer, E., and James Meacham. 2016. The Sacred Mountain Shiveet Khairkhan (Bayan Ölgiy aimag, Mongolia) and the Centering of Cultural Indicators in the Age of Nomadic Pastoralism. *Annals of the American Association of Geographers* 2016: 1–12.

Jacobson-Tepfer, E., James Meacham, and Gary Tepfer. 2010. *Archaeology and Landscape in the Mongolian Altai: An Atlas*. ESRI Press, Redlands, CA.

Janz, Lisa, Robert G. Elston, and S. Burr George. 2009. Dating North Asian Surface Assemblages with Ostrich Eggshell: Implications for Palaeoecology and Extirpation. *Journal of Archaeological Science* 36, 9: 1982–1989.

Janz, Lisa, D. Odsuren, and D. Bukhchuluun. 2017. Transitions in Palaeoecology and Technology: Hunter-Gatherers and Early Herders in the Gobi Desert. *Journal of World Prehistory* 30:1–80.

Jones, Andrew Meirion, Davina Freeman, Blaze O'Connor, Hugo Lamdin-Whymark, Richard Tipping, and Aaron Watson. 2011. *An Animate Landscape: Rock Art and the Prehistory of Kilmartin, Argyll, Scotland.* Oxford: Windgather Press.

Kortum, D. Richard. 2018. *Ceremony in Stone.* Nepko Publishing, Ulaanbaatar.

Kovalev, A. A. ed. 2015. *Drevneishie Evropeitsy v Serdtse Azii: Chemurchekskii Kul'turnyi Fenomen.* Part II. St. Petersburg State Museum, St. Petersburg.

Kuzmin, Yaroslav. 2010. Extinction of the Woolly Mammoth (*Mammuthus primigenius*) and Wooly Rhinoceros (*Coelodonta antiquitatis*) in Eurasia: Review of Chronological and Environmental Issues. *Boreas* 39: 247–261.

Leslie, David M., Jr., and George B. Schaller. 2009. *Bos grunniens* and *Bos mutus* (Artiodactyla: Bovidae), *Mammalian Species* 836: 1–17.

MAIC (Mongolian Altai Inventory Collection). Digital Collections, University of Oregon Libraries. https://oregondigital.org/sets/maic.

Martin, Paul S. 1982. The Pattern and Meaning of Holoarctic Mammoth Extinction. In: Hopkins, David (Ed.), *Paleoecology of Beringia.* Academic Press, New York, London, pp. 399–408.

Miehe, Georg, Frank Schlütz, Sabine Miehe, et al. 2007. Mountain Forest Islands and Holocene Environmental Changes in Central Asia: A Case Study from the Southern Gobi Altay, Mongolia. *Palaeogeography, Palaeoclimatology, Palaeoecology* 250: 150–166.

Müller-Beck, H. 1982. Late Pleistocene Man in Northern Alaska and the Mammoth-Steppe Biome. In Hopkins, David (Ed.), *Paleoecology of Beringia.* Academic Press, New York, London, pp. 329–352.

Okladnikov, A. P. 1959. *Shishkinskiye pisanitsy, pamyatnik drevney kul'tury Pribaykal'ya.* Irkutskoye knizhnoye izd-vo, Moscow.

Okladnikov, A. P. 1972. *Tsentral'noasiatskiy ochag pervobytnogo iskusstva.* Nauka, Novosibirsk.

Okladnikov, A. P. 1981. *Petroglify Chulutyn-Gola (Mongoliya).* Nauka, Novosibirsk.

Okladnikov, A. P., Ye. A. Okladnikova, V. D. Zaparozhskaya, and Ye. A. Skorynina. 1979. *Petroglify doliny reki Yelangash.* Nauka, Novosibirsk.

Okladnikov, A. P., Ye. A. Okladnikova, V. D. Zaparozhskaya, and Ye. A. Skorina. 1980. *Petroglify Gornogo Altaya*. Novosibirsk: Nauka.

Okladnikov, A. P., Ye. A. Okladnikova, V. D. Zaparozhskaya, and Ye. A. Skorina. 1982. *Petroglify urochishcha Sary-Sartak*. Novosibirsk: Nauka.

Orlova, Lyobov A., Yaroslav V. Kuzmin, and Vyacheslav N. Demenitev. 2004. A Review of the Evidence for Extinction Chronologies for Five Species of Upper Pleistocene Megafauna in Siberia. *Radiocarbon* 46, 1: 301–314.

Rhode, David, David B. Madsen, P. Jeffrey Brantingham, and Tsultrim Dargye. 2007. Yaks, Yak Dung, and Prehistoric Human Habitation of the Tibetan Plateau. In: Madsen, D. B., Chen, F. H., and Gao, X. (Eds.), *Late Quaternary Climate Change and Human Adaptation in Arid China*. Amsterdam, Boston, London: Elsevier. Developments in Quaternary Science, Vol. 9, pp. 205–224.

Roberts, Richard G. 2017. Optical Dating of Rock Art. In: David, Bruno, and McNiven, Ian J. (Eds.), *The Oxford Handbook of the Archaeology and Anthropology of Rock Art*. Oxford Handbooks Online, Oxford.

Rudaya, Natalia, Pavel Tarasov, Nadezhda Dorofeyuk, et al. 2009. Holocene Environments and Climate in the Mongolian Altai Reconstructed from the Hoton-Nur Pollen and Diatom Records: A Step towards Better Understanding Climate Dynamics in Central Asia. *Quaternary Science Reviews* 28: 540–554.

Sapozhnikov V. V. 1949. *Po Russkomu i Mongol'skomu Altayu*. V. V. Obruchev, ed. State Geographical Literature, Moscow.

Shahgedanova, Maria, Nikolay Mikhailov, Sergey Larin, and Aleksandr Bredikhin. 2002. The Mountains of Southern Siberia. In: Shahgedanov, Maria (Ed.), *The Physical Geography of Northern Eurasia*. Oxford University Press, Oxford, pp. 314–349.

Tarasov, P., N. Dorofeyuk, and E. Metel'tseva. 2000. Holocene Vegetation and Climate Changes in Hoton-Nuur Basin, Northwest Mongolia. *Boreas* 29: 117–126.

Tarasov, P., D. Jolly, and J. O. Kaplan. 1997. A Continuous Late Glacial and Holocene Record of Vegetation Changes in Kazakhstan. *Palaeogeography, Palaeoclimatology, Palaeoecology* 136: 281–292.

Tseveendorzh, D., V. D. Kubarev, and E. Yakobson (Jacobson). 2005. *Aral Tolgoin Khadny Zurag*. Institute of Archaology, Mongolian Academy of Sciences, Ulaanbaatar.

Vartanyan S. L., V. E. Garutt, and A. V. Sher. 1993. Holocene Dwarf Mammoths from Wrangel Island in the Siberian Arctic. *Nature* 262: 337–340.

Velichko, A. A., H. E. Wright, C. W. Barnofsky, eds. 1984. *Late Quaternary Environments of the Soviet Union*. University of Minnesota Press, Minneapolis.

Velichko, A. A., and E. M. Zelikson. 2005. Landscape, Climate and Mammoth Food Resources in the East European Plain during the Late Paleolithic Epoch. *Quaternary International* 126–128: 137–151.

Vershchagin N. K., and G. F. Baryshnikov. 1982. Paleoecology of the Mammoth Fauna in the Eurasian Arctic. In: Hopkins, David (Ed.), *Paleoecology of Beringia*. Academic Press, New York, London, pp. 267–279.

Wallace, V. A. 2015. Buddhist Sacred Mountains, Auspicious Landscapes, and Their Agency. In Wallace, V. A. (Ed.), *Buddhism in Mongolian History, Culture, and Society*. Oxford University Press, Oxford, pp. 221–240.

Zhao, Y., Z. Yu, F.-H. Chen, and C. An. 2007. Holocene Vegetation and Climate Changes from Fossil Pollen Records in Arid and Semi-arid China. In: Madsen, D. B., Chen, F. H., and Gao, X. (Eds.), *Late Quaternary Climate Change and Human Adaptation in Arid China*. Amsterdam, Boston, London: Elsevier. Developments in Quaternary Science, Vol. 9, pp. 51–65.

Cambridge Elements ≡

Environmental Humanities

Louise Westling

University of Oregon

Louise Westling is an American scholar of literature and environmental humanities who was a founding member of the Association for the Study of Literature and Environment and its President in 1998. She has been active in the international movement for environmental cultural studies, teaching and writing on landscape imagery in literature, critical animal studies, biosemiotics, phenomenology, and deep history.

Serenella Iovino

University of North Carolina at Chapel Hill

Serenella Iovino is Professor of Italian Studies and Environmental Humanities at the University of North Carolina at Chapel Hill. She has written on a wide range of topics, including environmental ethics and ecocritical theory, bioregionalism and landscape studies, ecofeminism and posthumanism, comparative literature, eco-art, and the Anthropocene.

Timo Maran

University of Tartu

Timo Maran is an Estonian semiotician and poet. Maran is Professor of Ecosemiotics and Environmental Humanities and Head of the Department of Semiotics at the University of Tartu. His research interests are semiotic relations of nature and culture, Estonian nature writing, zoosemiotics and species conservation, semiotics of biological mimicry.

About the Series

The environmental humanities is a new transdisciplinary complex of approaches to the embeddedness of human life and culture in all the dynamics that characterize the life of the planet. These approaches reexamine our species' history in light of the intensifying awareness of drastic climate change and ongoing mass extinction. To engage this reality, *Cambridge Elements in Environmental Humanities* builds on the idea of a more hybrid and participatory mode of research and debate, connecting critical and creative fields.

Cambridge Elements ☰

Environmental Humanities

Elements in the Series

The Anatomy of Deep Time: Rock Art and Landscape in the Altai Mountains of Mongolia
Esther Jacobson-Tepfer

A full series listing is available at: www.cambridge.org/EIEH

Printed in the United States
By Bookmasters